KOREAN IN A HURRY

KOREAN in a HURRY

A Quick Approach to

Spoken Korean

(Revised Edition)

by

Samuel E. Martin

Professor of Far Eastern Linguistics
Yale University

Charles E. Tuttle Company
Rutland, Vermont & Tokyo, Japan

Published by
Charles E. Tuttle Company, Inc.
of Rutland, Vermont & Tokyo, Japan

Editorial Offices:
Suido 1-chome, 2-6
Bunkyo-ku, Tokyo

Library of Congress
Catalog Card No. 60-8363

International Standard Book No. 0-8048-0349-8

First edition, August, 1954
Second printing, September, 1954
Second (revised) edition, 1960
Thirty-fifth printing, 1993

PRINTED IN SINGAPORE

CONTENTS

(v)

INTRODUCTION

THIS BOOK has been written to fill a specific need: that of the thousands of foreign servicemen and civilians stationed in Korea for a year or two who wish to learn something of the language spoken around them. The structure of Korean is peculiarly complex, and difficulties plague the foreign student from the very beginning. I have attempted to simplify some of the common problems and to acquaint the reader with the most useful way to say a lot of everyday things.

The sentences are almost all given in the Polite (-ŏ yo) style, which is both the simplest and the most widely useful. From this style, another common style—the Intimate—is easily derived simply by dropping the final particle. Koreans who look at the book will miss the Formal (-sŭmnida) style which they feel more appropriate to use with foreigners on first acquaintance. My purpose in sticking to one style is to provide the reader with the means to say a great many different things, rather than teach him a great many ways to say the same thing. From an academic point of view, this approach has certain drawbacks. From the practical point of view, it is the quickest and simplest way to put the foreigner into direct communication with Koreans, and that is the aim of this book.

The material is presented in the original McCune-Reischauer Romanization so that it may be used in conjunction with Joan V. Underwood's *Concise English-Korean Dictionary Romanized.* This system contains a number of features which make the rather complicated structure of Korean grammar seem even more difficult than it is. The McCune-Reischauer Romanization is based on an attempt to use common English values of letters to represent Korean sounds in terms of the raw impressions they make on an American ear. This system was influenced by the Wade-Giles Romanization of Chinese and the Hepburn Romanization of Japanese. Both of these Romanizations have certain shortcomings (particularly the Chinese one), but the shortcomings do not stand out as sore thumbs in the way those of the McCune-Reischauer Romanization do, because the systems of sounds and sound changes of Chinese and Japanese are so much simpler than those of Korean. The excuse for using this rather cumbersome system here is that is seems to be favored by the person who has time for only a quick brush with the language. I have tried to simplify the use of the McCune-Reischauer system to some extent by generous word division and by showing automatic sound changes only within words. If the reader plans to go on with his study of Korean beyond the material contained in this book, he will probably find it advisable to do so either in the native script (**Han-gŭl**) or in one of the other Romanization systems shown in the table at the end of the lessons. For a scientific description of the structure of Korean, the reader is referred to the author's other publications, *Korean Phonemics* and *Korean Morphophonemics*. A comprehensive grammar is in preparation.

I hope that the material contained in this book—while perhaps oversimplifying a complicated language—will be of some immediate, practical use to the reader who wants to learn some Korean "in a hurry". And I hope some of those who learn Korean in a hurry will find such an interest in the language and the people who speak it that they will someday spare the time and patience needed to master the language.

Tokyo, August 1954   SAMUEL E. MARTIN

NOTE TO REVISED EDITION

Since work on a Korean-English dictionary has held up the preparation of my comprehensive grammar for the past several years, it seems a good idea to put out a new edition of this little book which has met with a kinder reception than I had anticipated. I am grateful to Professor Edward C. Wagner, of Harvard University, for pointing out a number of errors; these have been corrected in this edition. Several readers have asked where they might buy my monograph *Korean Morphophonemics;* it is available for $2.00 from the Secretary of the Linguistic Society of America, Box 7790, University Station, Austin 12, Texas. The article "Korean Phonemics" appears in the anthology *Readings in Linguistics*, edited by Martin Joos and available for $6.00 from the Columbia University Press, 2960 Broadway, New York 27, New York.

New Haven, November 1959   S.E.M.

KOREAN IN A HURRY

Lesson 1

VOWELS

The vowels and combinations of **y** or **w** with a vowel are pronounced somewhat as follows:

i		as Mar*i*ne (m*ee*t, ch*ea*t)
	wi	as *we* (q*uee*n, bet*wee*n, s*wee*t)
e		as m*e*t (or h*ey* s*ay* m*a*te)
	ye	as *yes* (or *yea* man.)
	we	as *wet* (or *way*, s*way*, q*uake*)
oe		usually pronounced just like **we**
ae		as *a*t (c*a*p, s*a*ck, h*a*m)
	yae	as *ya*m
	wae	as *Wa*c (sw*a*m)
a		as *ah* (h*ah*, f*a*ther)
	ya	as *ya*rd, German *ja*
	wa	as *Wah*shington (but not *Wor*shington or *Woh*shington!)
ŭ		as "j*i*st" (=just), "p*i*rty" (=pretty); or, as J*u*ne s*oo*n, t*oo*, c*oo*l WITH LIPS PULLED BACK HARD
u		as J*u*ne (s*oo*n, t*oo*,) WITH LIPS PUSHED OUT
	yu	as *you* (c*ue*, p*ew*) WITH LIPS PUSHED OUT
ɔ		between s*o*ng and s*u*ng; like s*o*ng (l*aw*, b*ough*t) WITH LIPS PULLED BACK HARD; or, like s*u*ng (l*u*ng, b*u*tt) WITH TONGUE PULLED BACK AND PUSHED DOWN (AS IF WITH A SPOON)

yŏ	between *yaw*n and *you*ng
wŏ	between *wa*ll and *wo*n
o	as n*o* (s*o*, P*o*go)
yo	as *yo*kel

NOTE: The combination **ŭi** has three different pronounciations:

(1) At the beginning of a word it is pronounced like **ŭ**.

(2) At the end of a word it is pronounced like **i**.

(3) But, the particle meaning *of* is pronounced like **e**.

In this book, you will find the first pronounciation indicated as **ŭ(i)**, and the second as **(ŭ)i**. But you will have to remember that the particle **ŭi** is pronounced **e**.

Here are some common words to practice the vowels on:

i	*tooth*	wae	*why*
chip	*house*	mal	*horse*
kwi	*ear*	pam	*night*
chwi	*rat*	yayu	*teasing*
twi	*behind*	wanja	*meatballs*
ne	*yes*	kwanggo	*advertisement*
ye	*yes*	ŭmsik	*food*
yebaedang	*church*	ŭnhaeng	*bank*
hoe	*meeting*	kŭrim	*picture*
Ch'oe	(*name*)	nun	*eye*
soe	*iron*	mu	*turnip*
sae	*bird*	yuri	*glass*
saekssi	*girl*	tubu	*bean-curd*
aegi	*baby*	kyuryul	*regulations*
hae	*sun ; year*	mŏnjŏ	*first of all*
maeil	*every day*	ŏnje	*when*
yaegi	*story, talk*	nŏmŏ	*too much*

(2)

kyŏngje	economics	p'yo	ticket
yŏmnyŏ	worry	hakkyo	school
wŏn	Yen	ŭ(i)ja	chair
hwŏnjaeng	quarrel	ŭ(i)sa	doctor
ton	money	ŭ(i)mi	meaning
sori	sound	chu(ŭ)i	attention
kong	ball	t'o(ŭ)i	discussion

Lesson 2

CONSONANTS

The consonants **m**, **n**, and **h** are pronounced much like English.

The consonant written **ng** is pronounced as in si*ng*, si*ng*er (but NOT as in English fi*ng*er which sounds like fi*ngg*er).

The consonants **p**, **t**, and **k** sound like weakly articulated English *p*in, *t*in, *k*in; but at the end of a syllable (hi*p*, hi*t*, hi*ck*) be careful not to give these consonants a special release—just shut the sound off.

The sounds written **p'**, **t'** and **k'** are said with a heavy puff of breath like English u*ph*eaval, pen*th*ouse, coo*kh*ouse.

The sounds written **pp**, **tt**, and **kk** are pronounced with the throat and mouth muscles very tense and released sharp with no puff of breath, a little like English s*p*y, s*t*ay, s*k*id.

P, **t**, and **k** are LAX; **p'**, **t'**, and **k'** are BREATHY;

and **pp**, **tt**, and **kk** are TENSE. In the same way **ch** is lax (as in English *church* weakly articulated), **ch'** is breathy (as in English bea*ch-h*ouse), and **tch** is tense.

You may hear **pp**, **tt**, **kk**, and **tch** like English *b*it, *d*ip, *g*o, and *J*oe—if you pronounce these words with a specially strong emphasis. But ordinarily English *b*, *d*, *g*, and *j* are rather weakly pronounced like the way Korean **p**, **t**, **k**, and **ch** sound between voiced sounds. We write these Korean sounds as **b**, **d**, **g**, and **j** when they occur between voiced sounds (the vowels, **m**, **n**, **l**) to remind you of this.

The Korean sound **s** is lax and sounds like a very weak English *s*—or, sometimes, especially in front of the vowel **i**, like English *sh*. The Korean sound **ss** is tense and sounds like a very emphatic English *s*. Don't worry if you can't hear the difference between these two; there are few situations in which you will be misunderstood if you confuse them.

The Korean sound which we write sometimes **l** and sometimes **r** is very difficult for Americans because it sounds like a number of different English sounds. Within a word when it sounds like the *l* in fi*ll* we write it **l**; when it sounds like the *r* in British be*rr*y (or the *t* in English Be*tt*y; or the Japanese *r*, or the single Spanish *r*) we write it **r**. Be careful to pronounce the Korean **mm**, **nn**, and **ll** as DOUBLE sounds: like English ge*m-m*aker, pe*n-kn*ife, we*ll-l*iked.

Here are some common words to practice the consonants.

pi	*rain*	**ppiru**	*beer*
p'i	*blood*	**pyŏ**	*rice plant*

p'yo	ticket	yukpun	six minutes
ppyŏ	bone	ch'imdae	berth, bunk
tal	moon	pando	peninsula
t'al	mask	talda	is sweet
ttal	daughter	ch'upta	is cold
to	province	chŏkta	is small
t'op	a saw	Yŏngguk	England
tto	again, yet	silgwa	fruit
ki	spirit, disposition	sip-ku	nineteen
k'i	height, size	namja	man, male
kki	a meal	hwanja	patient
kae	dog	maekchu	beer
k'al	knife	chong-i	paper
kkae	sesame	tong-an	interval
cho	millet	iri	this way
ch'o	candle	kŭrŏk'e	in that way, so
tchok	side, direction	resŭt'orang	restaurant
sal	flesh	radio	radio
ssal	uncooked rice	p'iryo	necessity
sŭnta	stands up	p'arwŏl	August
ssŭnta	writes	il	work, job
tambae	cigarettes	mul	water
kongbu	study	mullon	of course
Ilbon	Japan	ppalli	fast

Lesson 3

SOUND CHANGES

When you link words together without pausing between, certain sound changes take place. If the first word ends in a consonant and the second begins with

a vowel, the final consonant of the first word is pronounced as the initial consonant of the second word:

| sǒm_i | *island* (as subject) | =sǒ-mi |
| sǒm_e | *to the island* | =sǒ-me |

If the final consonant is **p**, **t**, **ch**, or **k** it changes in
sound to **b**, **d**, **j**, or **g**:

ch'aek_i	*book* (as subject)	ch'ae-gi
Han-guk_e	*to Korea*	Han-gu-ge
pap_i	*cooked rice* (as subject)	pa-bi
nach_e	*in the daytime*	na-je

If the final consonant is **l**, it changes in sound to *r*:

| il_i | *work* (as subject) | =i-ri |
| mul_ŭl | *water* (as object) | =mu-rŭl |

Now if the first word ends in a voiced sound (a
vowel, or **m**, **n**, **ng**, or **l**) and the second word begins
with **p**, **t**, **ch**, or **k**, this changes to **b**, **d**, **j**, or **g**:

Ilbon_to	*Japan too*	Il-bon-do
ch'aek_ie_yo	*it's a book*	ch'ae-gi-e-yo
i_kǒ_pose_yo	*just look at this*	i-gǒ-bo-se-yo
kǔ_taŭm	*next to that*	kǔ-da-ŭm
kǔ_chǒn_e	*before that*	kǔ-jǒ-ne

If the second word begins with **m** or **n** and the first
word ends in **p**, **t**, or **k**, these change to **m**, **n**, and
ng respectively:

chip_mada	*every house*	chim-ma-da
mot_mǒgǒ	*can't eat*	mon-mǒ-gǒ
ch'aek_mada	*every book*	ch'aeng-ma-da

The combinations **tp**, **ts**, and **tk** usually sound like **pp**, **ss**, and **kk**:

mot‿pwa‿yo	*can't see*	mo-ppwa-yo
mot‿sa‿yo	*can't buy*	mo-ssa-yo
mot‿ka‿yo	*can't go*	mo-kka-yo

At the end of a word before a pause or another consonant, the only consonants which occur are **p**, **t**, **k**, **m**, **n**, **ng**, and **l**. But there are a few words which have basic forms (the forms you hear when linked with a following word beginning with a vowel) in other consonant combinations. These are changed as follows (see also Lesson 17):

BEFORE VOWEL	BEFORE PAUSE OR CONSONANT
P'	**P**
ap'‿e *in front*	ap *front*; ap‿to *front too*
PS	**P**
kaps‿i *price* (subj.)	kap *price*; kap‿to *price too*
S	**T**
os‿ŭl *clothes* (object)	ot *clothes*; ot‿to *clothes too*
T'	**T**
pat'‿ŭn *garden* (topic)	pat *garden*; pat‿to *garden too*
CH'	**T**
kkoch'‿ŭn *flower* (topic)	kkot *flower*; kkot‿to *flower too*
CH	**T**
nach‿e *in the day-time*	nat *daytime*; nat‿to *daytime too*
KK	**K**
pakk‿e *outside*	pak *outside*; pak‿to *outside too*
LK	**K**
talk‿i *chicken* (subj.)	tak *chicken*; tak‿to *chicken too*

There are certain other sound changes which are less regular. You may also notice sound variants.

Sometimes the same thing will be pronounced in two different ways even by the same speaker. The most common of these is the dropping of **h** between voiced sounds:

man(h)i	*lots*	**annyong(h)i**	*peacefully*
pang(h)ak	*school vacation*	**ŭn(h)aeng**	*bank*
a(h)op	*nine*		

You may also notice that **w** sometimes drops, especially after **p, p', pp, m, u, o**:

chŏm(w)ŏn	*clerk*	**sam(w)ŏl**	*March*
ku(w)ŏl	*September*	**o(w)ŏl**	*May*

One irregular sound change which is quite common is the replacement of an initial **p, t, ch, s,** or **k** by their tense counterparts **pp, tt, tch, ss,** or **kk**. In this book, the "reinforcement" of the initial sound is sometimes shown with parentheses: **(p)p, (t)t, (t)ch, (s)s,** or **(k)k**. For example:

oje(p)pam *last night*   **yŏl-(t)tul** *twelve*

NOTE 1: It is important to remember that **b, d, j, g,** and **r** are just positional variants of **p, t, ch, k,** and **l** respectively. **B** and **p** function as one sound unit in the structure of Korean and the native script (**Han-gŭl**) writes both with the same symbol. This is true also for **d** and **t, j,** and **ch, g** and **k, r** and **l** respectively. So when we speak of an ending beginning with **t**, it goes without saying we mean to add "(and this changes to **d** automatically between voiced sounds)."

NOTE 2: Common linking of words is shown in the first half of the book with the mark‿. In later lessons this mark is omitted. You will, of course, sometimes hear linking in places other than those shown here.

Lesson 4

NAMES AND GREETINGS

Kim sŏnsaeng, annyŏng hasimnikka ?	*How are you, Mr. Kim ? (Are you well, Mr. Kim ?)*
Ne. Komapsŭmnida.	*(Yes=) fine, thank you.*
I puin, annyŏng hasimnikka ?	*How are you, Mrs. Lee ?*
Yongsŏ hasipsio.	*Excuse me.*
Mian hamnida.	*I'm sorry.*
Sille haessŭmnida.	*Excuse me (for something I did).*
Sille hamnida.	*Excuse me (for something I am doing).*
Sille hagessŭmnida.	*Excuse me (for something I am going to do).*
Ch'ŏn man ŭi malssum imnida.	*(Its one in 10 million words=) Not at all. Think nothing of it.*
Kwaench'anssŭmnikka ? Chossŭmnikka ?	*Is it all right ? May I ?*
Kwaench'anssŭmnida.	*It makes no difference ; it's OK ; you may.*
Chossŭmnida.	*It's all right ; it's good ; it's fine ; you may.*
Ŏsŏ tŭrŏ osipsio.	*Come right in.*
Tto poepkessŭmnida.	*See you later. So long.*

Sayang‿ch'i masipsio.	*Go right ahead. Don't stand on ceremony. Help yourself. Make yourself comfortable. Don't hesitate. Any time at all. Please feel free to (call on me, take what you want, eat all you can, do what you please, etc.).*
Annyŏng-(h)i kasipsio.	*Goodbye (to one who is leaving).*
Annyŏng-(h)i kesipsio.	*Goodbye (to one who is staying).*

A Korean has two names: the family name is followed by a personal name. Most of the family names are of one syllable like **Pak, Paek, Ch'oe, Chang, Min, Yu, Im,** but a few unusual ones have two syllables like **Hwangbo.** If the family name has one syllable, the personal name has two: **I Sŭngman** (Syngman Rhee). **Kim Il(s)sŏng** (Kim Ilsung). If the family name has two syllables, the personal name has only one, so that either way there are three syllables in the full name. This system, together with most of the names themselves, was borrowed from China. Some names are exceptions to this system.

The word **sŏnsaeng** has two meanings: one is *teacher*, the other is a title which can be translated *Mr., Mrs.,* or *Miss* depending on whom you are talking about. For *Mrs.* you can also say **puin** which means *lady* or *wife*. There is a word for *you* (**tangsin**) but instead of using it the Koreans usually refer to a person either by title and name: **Kim sŏnsaeng** *You* (, *Mr. Kim*), or just by title: **sŏnsaeng** *You* (, *sir*). To make this more polite the word **nim** is often added: **sŏnsaeng‿nim.**

The word for *I, me* is **na**; for *my* **nae.** For *he* or *she* you say **kŭ‿saram** or **kŭ‿i** *that person*; for *his* or *hers* you say **kŭ‿saram‿ŭi** *of that person* or just **kŭ.** For *they, them* you can say either **kŭ‿saram** or **kŭ‿saram‿tŭl** (also **kŭ‿i, kŭ‿i‿tŭl**). For *their,* **kŭ‿saram‿ŭi** or **kŭ‿saram‿tŭl‿ŭi.** **Uri** means *we* or *our* but sometimes it translates into English *me* or *my.*

You will notice that many common expressions have meanings which seem different from their literal translations. These literal translations are intended only as a help in remembering the words in the expressions.

Lesson 5

SENTENCE STRUCTURE

English sentences seem to tell you a lot more about a given situation than their equivalents in Korean. That is because the Korean likes to leave out any details that seem obvious from the context or the situation. It's a rare English sentence that has no subject, but we use such sentences in telegrams (*Having fine time. Wish you were here.*) and in commands (*Keep off the grass. Send more money.*). In Korean it is quite common to omit the subject, and often many other parts of the equivalent English sentence, too. You'll often wonder why the Korean words for *some*, *any*, *it* and other common little English expressions seldom appear in the Korean versions of examples.

A Korean sentence is quite complete with nothing but a verb :

Hamnida.	*(Someone) does (something).*

If the Korean want to supply further details about the situation, he puts them in before the verb. For example, if he wants to tell just what kind of an action the 'does' refers to :

Kongbu‿hamnida.	*(Someone) does* STUDYING = *studies (something).*

If it seems important to add the object of the action :

Han-guk‿mal‿ŭl kongbu‿ hamnida.	*(Someone) studies* KOREAN.

And the place :

Hakkyo‿sŏ Han-guk‿mal‿ ŭl kongbu‿hamnida.	*(Someone) studies Korean* IN SCHOOL.

And the time :

Chigŭm hakkyo‿sŏ Han-guk ‿mal‿ŭl‿kongbu hamnida.	*(Someone) studies Korean in school* NOW.

And the subject of the action (the actor) :

Haksaeng‿i chigŭm hakkyo ‿sŏ Han-guk‿mal‿ŭl kongbu hamnida.	*THE STUDENT studies Korean in school now.*

(12)

The order in which you put the additional information like object, place, time, and subject depends largely on the importance of the information. The indispensable news in every sentence is the verb—this goes at the end. As a general rule, the farther you get away from the end of the sentence, the more dispensable the information you are supplying.

In other words, if you wanted to say the same thing a little more briefly, you'd likely chop off the earlier parts of the sentence first. Since sometimes the SUBJECT is so well known you don't have to mention it, but at other times it's the OBJECT—or the place, or the time, or something else—there isn't any fixed order. If all other things are equal—that is, if you're equally in the dark about subject and object—it's usually better to keep the object near the verb.

Lesson 6

SOME USEFUL EXPRESSIONS

Asigessŭmnikka ? ⎫ 'Ihae hasimnikka ? ⎭	*Do you understand ?*
Ne.	*Yes.* (Often pronounced **ye** in the South.)
Ani.	*No.*
Ani yo.	*No.* (More polite)
Amnida.	*I understand.*
Morŭmnida.	*I don't understand.*

(13)

Han ‿ pŏn ‿ to hae chu-sipsio.	*Please say it again.*
Ch'ŏnch'ŏn-(h)i hae chu-sipsio.	*Please say it slowly.*
Ch'aek ‿ ŭl posipsio.	*Please look at your book.*
Ch'aek ‿ ŭl poji masi-psio.	*Please don't look at your book.*
Han-guk ‿ mal ‿ lo hasi-psio.	*Please talk in Korean.*
Yŏng-ŏ ‿ ro haji masi-psio.	*Please don't talk in English.*
Kach'i hasipsida.	*Let's do it (say it) together.*
Ta kach'i.	*All together.*
Tŭtki ‿ man hasipsio.	*Just listen please.*
Kŭrŏssŭmnikka ?	*Is that so? Oh? Really?*
Kŭrŏssŭmnida.	*That's so. Yes. That's it.*
Kŭrŏch'i ‿ man......	*But...... However......*
Kŭrigo......	*And (in addition)......*
Kŭrae ‿ sŏ......	*And so...... So......*
......katta chusipsio.	*Please bring me.......*

Lesson 7

MORE USEFUL EXPRESSIONS

Ppalli kasipsio.	*Please go fast.*
Ch'ŏnch'ŏn-(h)i kasip-sio.	*Please go slow.*
Parŭn p'yŏn ‿ ŭro.	*To the right.*
Oen p'yŏn ‿ ŭro.	*To the left.*
Paro ap' ‿ ŭro.	*Straight ahead.*

Yŏgi.	Here (*near me or us*). *This place.*
Kŏgi.	*There (near you). That place.*
Chŏgi.	*Over there (away from you and me). That place over there.*
Iri_ro or Yori_ro.	*This way.*
Kŭri_ro or kori_ro.	*That way.*
Chŏri_ro or Chori_ro.	*That way over there.*
Iri osipsio.	*Please come this way.*
I_kŏ(t).	*This (thing).* DON'T FORGET *k* SOUNDS LIKE *g* WHEN LINKED WITH VOICED SOUNDS.
Kŭ_kŏ(t).	*That (thing).*
Chŏ_kŏ(t).	*That (thing) over there.*
Ŏdi ?	*Where ? What place ?*
M(u)ŏ(t) ?	*What ?* (Pronounced **muŏt, muŏ, mŏt,** or **mŏ.**)
Wae ?	*Why ?*
Ŏnje ?	*When ?*
Chigŭm.	*Now.* (Also pronounced **chikkŭm.**)
Onŭl.	*Today.*
Naeil.	*Tomorrow.*
Ŏje.	*Yesterday.*
I_taŭm.	*Next (after this).*
Kŭ_taŭm.	*Next (after that).*
I_hu.	*Later (after this).*
Kŭ_hu.	*Later (after that).*
Kŭ_chŏn.	*Before that.* DON'T FORGET *ch* SOUNDS LIKE *j* WHEN LINKED WITH VOICED SOUNDS.
Pŏlssŏ.	*Already.*
Ajik.	*Not yet.*
Chom.	*A little.*
Chom tŏ.	*A little more.*
Tŏ.	*More.*
Chom chusipsio.	*Give me a little please.*

Chom tŏ chusipsio.	*Please give me a little more.*
Chom-ch'ŏrŏm.	*Seldom.*
Chajo	*Often.*
Nŏmu.	*Too much.*
Nŏngnŏk.	*Enough.*
Manhi.	*Lots.*
Ta.	*All.*
Chal.	(1) *Well.* (2) *Lots.* (3) *Often.*
Ch'am.	*Real. Very. Quite.*

Lesson 8

"IS" AND "HAS"

There are two verbs which translate the English words *is, am, are, be* in Korean: **isse⌣yo** *exists, stays* and **ie⌣yo** *equals.* You use **ie⌣yo** when you have a sentence which can be reduced to the formula $A=B$:

$\overset{A}{This}$ $\overset{}{\text{IS}}$ $\overset{B}{a\ book.}$	$\overset{A}{\text{I⌣kŏ,}}$ $\overset{B}{\text{ch'aek⌣ie⌣yo.}}$

Notice that the formula has to change in Korean because the verb always comes at the end. The verb expression **ie⌣yo** is peculiar in a number of ways: (1) It always has something in front of it, with which it is linked in pronunciation. (Other verbs can make a complete sentence by themselves.) (2) It drops the vowel **i** after a word ending in a vowel. We will

(16)

show the abbreviation of this vowel by a hyphen:

Kŭ͡ kŏ, chapchi͡ -e͡ yo.	*That is a magazine.*
Kich'a͡ -e͡ yo.	*(It)'s a train.*
Muŏ͡ -e͡ yo?	*What is (it)?*
Pihaenggi͡ -e͡ yo.	*It's an airplane.*
Nugu͡ -e͡ yo?	*Who is it?*
Na͡ -e͡ yo.	*It's me.*
Kŭ͡ saram, nugu͡ -e͡ yo?	*Who is that person? Who is he?*
I͡ saram, nae ch'in-gu͡ -e͡ yo.	*This person is my friend.*
Hakkyo sŏnsaeng ͡ ie ͡ yo.	*He's a school teacher.*
Han-guk ͡ (s)saram ͡ ie ͡ yo?	*Is he a Korean (person)?*
Ani yo. Miguk ͡ (s)saram ͡ ie͡ yo.	*No. He's an American (person).*
Yŏgi, ŏdi͡ -e͡ yo?	*What place is this place?*
Yŏgi, yŏgwan ͡ ie͡ yo.	*This (place) is a hotel.*
Chŏgi, chŏnggŏjang ͡ ie ͡ yo.	*(That place) over there is a railroad station.*
Pihaengjang, ŏdi͡ -e͡ yo?	*Where (what place) is the airfield?*
Chŏgi͡ -e͡ yo.	*It's (that place) over there.*

Whenever *is* refers merely to EXISTENCE or to LOCATION rather than to IDENTIFICATION, you use isse͡ yo:

Ton ͡ (i), isse͡ yo?	*Is there any money?*
Ŏdi isse͡ yo?	*Where is it?*
Chungguk ͡ (s)saram ͡ (i), ŏdi isse͡ yo?	*Where's the Chinese (person)?*

This is the ordinary way of saying *has* or *got*: *I've got a cat.* = *There exists a cat.*

Kwaeng-i‿(ga), isse‿yo.	(Someone) has a cat.
Kim‿sŏnsaeng, chadong-ch'a‿(ga) isse‿yo?	Do you have an automobile, Mr. Kim?
Ani‿yo. Chajŏn-gŏ‿man isse‿yo.	No, I have only a bicycle.

To say *does not have* or *hasn't got* you use the verb expression **ŏpse‿yo**:

Sigan‿(i) ŏpse‿yo.	There isn't time = I haven't any time.
Ton‿(i) ŏpse‿yo.	I haven't any money.
Sige‿(ga) ŏpse‿yo?	Haven't you got a watch (clock)?
Ai‿(ga) ŏpse‿yo?	Don't you have any children?
Ttal‿man isse‿yo.	I have only a daughter.
Adŭl‿to isse‿yo.	I have a son too.

Lesson 9

MILITARY RANKS

To specify the branch of service the word **yukkun** *Army*, **haegun** *Navy*, or **konggun** *Air Force* precedes a person's rank:

Haegun Sowi	Ensign
Yukkun Sowi	2d Lieutenant
Konggun Sowi	2d Lieutenant (Air Force)
Changgyo	Officer
Changgun	Commanding General
Taejang	General, Admiral

Chungjang	*Lt. General, Vice Admiral*
Sojang	*Brigadier General, Rear Admiral*
Taeryŏng	*Colonel, Captain*
Chungnyŏng	*Lt. Colonel, Commander*
Soryŏng	*Major, Lt. Commander*
Taewi	*Captain, Lieutenant*
Chungwi	*1st Lieutenant, Lieutenant (junior grade)*
Sowi	*2d Lieutenant, Ensign*
Pyŏngsa ⎱ Pyŏng ⎰	*Army enlisted man*
Subyŏng	*Navy enlisted man*
Hasagwan	*Non-commissioned officer, Petty officer*
Sangsa	*Sergeant*
Tŭngmu sangsa	*First sergant*
Ilttŭng sangsa	*Master sergeant*
Idŭng sangsa	*Sergeant 1st class*
Hasa	*Corporal*
Ilttŭng pyŏng	*Private First Class*
Pyŏngjŏl	*Private*

Lesson 10

STYLES OF SPEECH

Each Korean sentence can be said in many different ways, depending on who is talking to whom. In America, even if you divide the people up into folks, swells, and snobs, you still talk much the same way to anyone. But a Korean uses different verb forms at the end of his sentence for different people he talks to. The system is quite complicated, and as a foreigner you won't be expected to get the hang of it right away.

In this book most of the sentences are in the POLITE or **yo** style, because this is the simplest to learn, and it is also the most generally useful. Some of the sentences, especially set greetings, are given in the FORMAL or **-sŭmnida** style.

Since you will hear a lot of the other styles, too, you had better know a little about them. In some of the styles there are different endings depending on whether your sentence is a STATEMENT, QUESTION, COMMAND or PROPOSITION. But in others, like the polite style, these are all the same, and you show the difference by intonation.

In making a command or proposition, Koreans often use the formal style even though they would ordinarily be talking to the person in the polite style— it's like adding '*please*' in English. On the next page is a list of some of the endings characteristic of the various styles.

The use of these styles is somewhat like this. You use the *formal* style to persons of higher status than you, and also to other people in formal situations. To strangers, you use the formal style until the "ice" is broken—after that, the polite style.

You use the *intimate* style (which is just the polite style with the polite particle **yo** dropped) with close friends and relatives, often mixing it with plain style.

You use the *plain* style in talking to children, and

sometimes with close friends and relatives. You use the *quotation* style (which is almost identical with the plain) when you are quoting what someone has said ; or when writing an article or book.

The *familiar* or " buddy-buddy " style is used by chums, especially young men, soldier buddies, school pals, etc.

The *authoritative* style is used by a person taking command of a situation : a policeman to a traffic offender, a customer to a laundryman, a guest to a hotel clerk, a passenger in a taxi. But should you be in any of these situations you certainly won't cause any hard feelings by using the polite style.

STYLE	STATEMENT	QUESTION	COMMAND	PROPOSITION
Formal	-sŭmnida	-sŭmnikka		
	-ŭmnida	-ŭmnikka	-ŭsipsio	-usipsida
	-mnida	-mnikka	-sipsio	-sipsida
Plain	-nŭnda	-ni	-ŏ‿ra	-cha, -ja
	-nda			
	-ta, -da			
Quotation	AS ABOVE	-nŭn‿ya	-ŭra	AS ABOVE
			-ra	
Familiar	-ne	-na	-ke, -ge‿(na)	-se
Authori- tative	-so -ŭo -o		-ŭsio -sio	-ŭpsida -psida
Intimate	-ŏ, -a, -e, -ae			
Polite	-ŏ‿yo, -a‿yo, -e‿yo, -ae‿yo			

Speech styles are quite different from " honorifics ", discussed in Lesson 26.

See if you can identify the style of each of the following utterances just by their endings. Don't memorize the sentences:

Pi＿ga wassŭmnikka?	*Did it rain?*
Yŏgi＿sŏ Chungguk ŭmsik＿ŭl mogŭl＿ ssu isso?	*Can I eat (=be served) Chinese food here?*
Naeil tora wa＿yo.	*I'll come back tomorrow.*
Pang＿i ŏpso?	*Haven't you a (vacant) room?*
Ŏnje wanna?	*When did you get here?*
Chamkkan swija.	*Let's rest a minute.*
Yŏgi anjŏ＿ra.	*Sit here.*
I＿kŏt, pose＿yo.	*Look at this.*
Ppalli kasio.	*Please go fast.*
Chip＿e ose＿yo.	*Come to (my) house.*
Muŏt hani?	*What are you doing?*
Kach'i hase.	*Let's do it together.*
Chigŭm mogŏssŏ.	*I've just now eaten.*
Ku ch'aek＿ŭl pŏlssŏ posŏsso?	*Have you already seen (or read) that book?*
Iri oge.	*Come this way.*
Chŏnjaeng kŭ＿man twŏtta.	*The war has stopped.*
Pyŏnghwa＿ga ogennŭn＿ya?	*Will peace come?*
Chal kongbu handa.	*He studies hard.*
Kwaeng-i ippŭda.	*The cat is pretty.*
Nŏmŏ chŏkta.	*It's too small.*
K'umnikka?	*Is it large?*

Now learn these words, all of which are ways of
calling attention : *Hey!* (on the street); *Hello!* (on
the telephone); *Waiter!* (in a restaurant); *Clerk!* (in
a store).   They are arranged here in order of politeness.   These words are derived from the expression
Yŏgi posipsio *look here:*

Yŏ-bo! (least polite ; can be rude)
Yŏ-bosio! (used in restaurants, stores, etc.)
Yŏ-bose yo! (most common, used anywhere)
Yŏ-bosipsio! (most polite)

Lesson 11

SOME HANDY NOUNS

Korean nouns occur in four different types of construction :

(1) Followed by a PARTICLE (Lessons 13, 14, 15) which shows the grammatical relationship of the noun to the rest of the sentence—whether it is the subject or object or place of the action.

Hakkyo‿ga k'ŏ‿yo.	*The school is big.*
Hakkyo‿rŭl pwa‿yo.	*I see the school.*
Hakkyo‿sŏ kongbu hae‿yo.	*I study at school.*

(2) Followed by the verb **ie‿yo** *equals* : is (Lesson 8) as the B part of the formula $(A)=B$.

(Kŭ chip) hakkyo‿-e‿yo.   *That (building) is a school.*

(3) Before another noun or a noun phrase which it modifies (describes).

Hakkyo sŏnsaeng.   *A school teacher.*

(4) All by itself, in an absolute construction,

usually followed by a pause.

> **Hakkyo, ŏdi isse yo?** *Where is there a school?*
> **Hakkyo kase yo?** *Are you going to school?*

A Korean noun like **ch'aek** *book* means all of these :
a book, some books, any books, the books. You usually have to tell from context whether the noun is
plural, definite, or what not. There is a plural indicator **tŭl** *group* often added at the end of a noun
or noun phrase, but you can't count on it. **Ch'aek
tŭl** means *books* but then so does **ch'aek** all by itself.

Here are some handy common nouns :

yŏnp'il	*pencil*	kongjang	*factory*
chong(-)i	*paper*	samusil	*office*
mannyŏnp'il	*fountain pen*	sang	*table*
sinmun	*newspaper*	ch'aek-sang	*desk*
tambae	*cigarettes*	ŭ(i)ja	*chair*
sŏngnyang	*matches*	pyŏnso	*toilet*
kabang	*briefcase, suit- case, hand- bag*	chumŏni	*pocket*
		pul	*light*
		mul	*water*
kongch'aek	*notebook*	sul	*liquor*
chip	*house, building*	pinu	*soap*
		sugŏn	*towel*
maejŏm	*stand, small shop*	wais(y)assŭ s(y)assŭ }	*shirt*
sangjŏm	*store*	paji	*trousers*
chang, sijang	*market*	yangmal	*socks*
		kudu	*shoes*
up'yŏn-guk	*postoffice*	oet'u	*overcoat*
ŭmsikchŏm	*restaurant*	moja	*hat*

Lesson 12

MORE HANDY NOUNS

Han-guk	} *Korea*	Minju-ju(ŭ)i	*Democracy*
Chosŏn		namja	*man, male, boy*
Puk Chosŏn	*North Korea*	yŏja	*woman, girl*
Nam Chosŏn	*South Korea*	kunin	*serviceman*
Chungguk	*China*	pyŏng	
Nosŏ	*Russia*	pyŏngjŏng	} *soldier*
Ssoryŏn	*Soviet Union*	sŏn-gyosa	*missionary*
Ilbon	*Japan*	moksa	*pastor, Rev-*
Miguk	*America*		*erend*
T'oigi	*Turkey*	changsa	*businessman,*
K'anada	*Canada*		*merchant*
Hoju	*Australia*	chŏmwŏn	*clerk (in store)*
T'aeguk	*Thailand*	samuwŏn	*clerk (in office)*
Indo	*India*	namp'yŏn	*husband*
Kurap'a	*Europe*	an(h)ae	*(one's own)*
Yŏngguk	*England*		*wife*
Kongsan-ju(ŭ)i	*Communism*	puin	*(someone else's)*
			wife
Kongsan-ju(ŭ)i-ja	*Communist* *(person)*	chikkong	*factory worker*
		nongbu	*farmer*

Lesson 13

PARTICLES

A PARTICLE is a little word which shows the relationship between the word or phrase preceding it and the rest of the sentence. Some Korean particles are similar in function to English prepositions (*in, on, at, from, till, of*); others indicate grammatical relationships which English shows by word order—like subject and object.

In English it makes a difference whether we say *The cat eats the bird* or *The bird eats the cat*. But in Korean the *cat* (**kwaengi**) and the *bird* (**sae**) can come in either order with either meaning: **Kwaengi, sae, mŏgŏ‿yo** means either *The cat eats the bird* or *The bird eats the cat*. And both meanings hold for **Sae, kwaengi, mŏgŏ‿yo** too.

The order in which we put the two nouns is determined by EMPHASIS rather than by which one does the eating. In order to make it clear which is the SUBJECT (which one eats) and which is the OBJECT (which one gets eaten), the Korean uses different particles: **Kwaengi‿GA sae‿RŬL mŏgŏ‿yo** and **Sae‿RŬL kwaengi‿GA mŏgŏ‿yo** both mean *The cat eats the bird*. **Sae‿GA kwaengi‿RŬL mŏgŏ‿yo** and also **Kwaengi‿RŬL sae‿GA mŏgŏ‿yo** both mean *The bird eats the cat*.

One characteristic of a particle is that you practically never pause in front of it—it's always linked with the proceding word. That's why we write here **ga** instead of **ka**, and **rŭl** instead of **lŭl**; these particles always sound this way. But we don't write **do** for **to** because this particle sometimes sounds like **to** and we like to spell a word the same way even when it changes sounds, so long as we can predict the changes automatically.

There are TWO-SHAPE particles and ONE-SHAPE particles. The one-shape particles always look the same, regardless of the word they follow. The two-shape particles have different shapes depending on the shape of the preceding word.

MEANING OF PARTICLE	SHAPE AFTER CONSONANT	SHAPE AFTER VOWEL
subject	i	ga
object	ŭl	rŭl
"*with, and*"	kwa	wa
"*or, and*"	ina	na
polite style	iyo	yo
"*hey! Oh!*" (vocative)	a	ya

Here are some examples with words of the preceding lessons:

PARTICLE	AFTER CONSONANT	AFTER VOWEL
subject	sŏngnyang‿i	tambae‿ga
	pang‿i	pyŏnso‿ga
	mul‿i (mu-ri)	pinu‿ga
object	yangmal‿ŭl	kudu‿rŭl
	sinmun‿ŭl	chongi‿rŭl
	sangjŏm‿ŭl	hakkyo‿rŭl
"*with, and*"	puin‿kwa*	an(h)ae‿wa
	pyŏngjŏng‿kwa*	sŏn-gyosa‿wa
	chikkong‿kwa*	nongbu‿wa
"*or, and, or the like*"	sugŏn‿ina	paji‿na
	ch'aek-sang‿ina	moja‿na
	chŏmwŏn‿ina	sowi‿na
polite style	Sŏnsaeng‿iyo! (*You!*)	Nugu yo? (*Who?*)
vocative	Kim‿sŏnsaeng‿a! (*Oh, Mr. Kim!*)	Kim‿moksa‿ya! (*Oh, Reverend Kim!*)
	Poktong‿a! (*Hey, Poktong!*)	Haksu‿ya! (*Hey, Haksu!*)

* Don't forget **k** sounds like **g** between voiced sounds.

(27)

NOTE: Before the subject particle, the following nouns have different shapes:

na	*I*	nae‿ga
chŏ	*I* (formal)	che‿ga
nugu	*who*	nu‿ga

Lesson 14

MORE PARTICLES

Here are some one-shape particles, with examples after both consonants and vowels:

PARTICLE	MEANINGS	EXAMPLES
ŭi (PRO-NOUNCED e)	modification or subordination,	Kim sŏnsaeng‿ŭi ch'aek‿ie‿yo. *It's Mr. Kim's book.* Nugu ŭi moja‿-e‿yo? *Whose hat is it?*
	(1) direction *to*	Hakkyo‿e ka‿yo. *He goes to school.* Ŭnhaeng‿e ka‿yo. *He goes to the bank.*
	(2) location *at, in*	Hakkyo‿e isse‿yo. *He is in school.* Ŭnhaeng‿e isse‿yo. *He's at the bank.*
	(3) a point in time *at, in*	Han‿si‿e wa‿yo. *I'm coming at 1 o'clock.* Ach'im‿e wa‿yo. *I'm coming in the morning.*

(28)

	(4) impersonal indirect object	**Ŭnhaeng_e ponae_yo.** *I'm sending (him, it) to the bank.* **Hoesa e p'yŏnji_rŭl ssŏ_yo.** *I'm writing a letter to the company.*
hant'e	personal indirect object *to, at, for (a person)*	**Sowi_hant'e ponae_yo.** *I'm sending it to the 2d Lt.* **Sŏnsaeng_hant'e ssŏ_yo.** *I'm writing to the teacher.*
ege	SAME; less colloquial	**Chungwi_ege chuŏ_yo.** *I'm giving it to the Lt.* **Chŏmwŏn _ege chuŏ_yo.** *I'm giving it to the clerk.*
pogo	SAME; more colloquial	**Nugu_pogo chŏnhwa hae_ yo?** *Who are you phoning (to)?* **Kim_sŏnsaeng_pogo chuŏ_yo.** *I'm giving it to Mr. Kim.*
sŏ, e_sŏ	(1) dynamic location, *(happens) at, in*	**Hakkyo_(e)_sŏ kongbu hae _yo.** *I study at school.* **Sŏul _(e)_sŏ il hae_yo.** *I work in Seoul.*
	(2) *from (a place)*	**Yŏgi_sŏ mŏrŏ_yo.** *It's far from here.* **Up'yŏnguk_e_ sŏ parŭn p'yŏn_ŭro kasipsio.** *From the postoffice, go to the right.*
ege_sŏ	*from (a person)*	**Nugu_ege_sŏ wasse yo?** *Who did it come from?* **Sŏnsaeng_ege_sŏ padŏsse yo.** *I got it from the teacher.*

put'ŏ	*from (a time or place)*	Yŏgi‿put'o sijak hapsida. *Let's start from here.* Ach'im ‿put'ŏ pam‿kkaji il hae‿ yo. *I work from morning till night.*
kkaji	*(all the way up) to (a place or time)*	Han‿si‿kkaji il hae‿yo. *I work till 1 o'clock.* Hakkyo ‿kkaji kach'i kapsita. *Let's go (as far as) to school together.*
hago	*with, and. (MORE COLLO- QUIAL THAN wa/kwa)*	Yŏnp'il‿hago chongi‿hago ch'aek‿i isse‿yo. *I've got pencil, paper, and books.* Ch'in-gu‿hago (kach'i) ka‿ yo. *I'm going (together) with a friend.*
man	*just, only*	Yŏnp'il‿man isse‿yo. *I've only got a pencil.* Chin-gu‿ man pwa‿yo. *I'm only seeing my friend.*
kach'i	*like*	Na‿kach'i hasipsio. *Do it like me.* Kŭ pyŏngjŏng‿ kach'i hasipsio. *Do it like that soldier.*
pakk‿e	*outside of, ex- cept for, aside from, or (any- thing) but*	Chip pakk‿e ŏpse‿yo. *I haven't but my house = I have only my house.* (Chip‿man isse‿yo). Kim‿moksa‿pakk‿e an‿ wasse‿yo. *(They) didn't come but Rev. Kim = Only Rev. Kim came.* (Kim‿moksa‿man wasse yo).

Lesson 15

SOME TRICKY PARTICLES

The 2-shape particle **ŭro/ro** has the shape **ro** after vowels, and **ŭro** after all consonants except **l**; after after **l** the shape is **lo**: **kich'a‿ro, parŭn p'yŏn‿ŭro, yŏnp'il‿lo.**

The meanings of the particle are as follows:

(1)	Manner *as*	**Pot'ong‿ŭro iltchŭgi wa‿yo.**	*He comes early as a usual thing.*
(2)	Function *as*	**Pyŏngjŏng‿ŭro Han-guk e wasse yo.**	*I came to Korea as a soldier.*
		Miguk yukkun chang-gyo‿ro Han-guk‿e isse‿yo.	*He's in Korea as an American army officer.*
(3)	State *is and*	**Kŭ yŏja‿nŭn Kim‿ sŏnsaeng‿(ŭi) ttal‿lo, Pusan‿e salgo isse‿yo.**	*That girl is Mr. Kim's daughter and is living in Pusan.*
(4)	Direction *toward, to*	**Oen p'yŏn ŭro kasipsio.**	*Go to the left.*
		Parŭn p'yŏn‿ŭro isse ‿yo.	*It's on (toward) the right.*
(5)	Means *with, by*	**I p'yŏnji‿rŭl yŏnp'il ‿lo ssŏ‿yo.**	*I'm writing this letter with a pencil.*
		Pihaenggi‿ro wasse‿ yo?	*Did you come by plane?*

The 2-shape particle **ŭn/nŭn** has the shape **ŭn** after consonants, **nŭn** after vowels: **chip‿ŭn, hakkyo‿nŭn.** The tricky thing about this particle is its meaning and use. As a tag translation you can try *as for*: as a tag meaning you can think of it as the TOPIC indicator.

What this particle does is take something and set it aside as a sort of stage-setting, as if to say—at the very beginning of your sentence—" Now this is what we're going to talk about." It is a particle of DE-EMPHASIS. The word or phrase in front of it refers to the least unknown ingredient in your communication—the part you'd be most likely to drop if you were going to send a telegram. For this reason, the phrase with this particle nearly always comes at the very beginning of the sentence. (Sometimes it is preceded by an adverb put out of place at the beginning for a kind of special emphasis.)

In Lesson 5 you learned that the important things in a Korean sentence tend to accumulate toward the END, and the less novel parts of your statement, the things the other fellow is more likely already to know, are put closer to the BEGINNING, where they are easier to drop. You also learned that, depending on the situation, the dispensable part of your news—what the other person probably knows already—may be the subject, the object, the place, the time, or anything EXCEPT THE VERB EXPRESSION.

So, if you want to take out any of the phrases in front of the verb and put them at the beginning in order to lessen the emphasis on them, you can then add the particle **ŭn/nŭn** to still further cut down their emphasis. When you do this to the subject or object, the ordinary particles (i/ga or ŭl/rŭl) do not occur.

For any other phrases, you can add the topic particle right after whatever particle would ordinarily be there. Let's take an example: **Kŭ haksaeng‿i chigŭm hakkyo‿sŏ Han-guk‿mal‿ŭl kongbu hae‿yo.** *That student is now studying Korean at school.* With differences of emphasis, this can be said in any of these ways:

Kŭ haksaeng‿ŭn chigŭm hakkyo‿sŏ Han-guk‿mal ‿ŭl kongbu hae‿yo. Chigŭm‿ŭn kŭ haksaeng‿ i hakkyo‿sŏ Han-guk‿mal‿ŭl kongbu hae‿yo. Hakkyo‿sŏ‿nŭn kŭ haksaeng‿i chigŭm Han-guk‿ mal‿ŭl kongbu hae‿yo. Han-guk‿mal‿ŭn kŭ haksaeng‿i chigŭm hakkyo‿sŏ kongbu hae‿yo.

But just how do you use this reduction of emphasis? It is used, for one thing, when you are making different statements about two different subjects or objects, de-emphasizing these in order to play up their points of CONTRAST:

Yŏgwan‿ŭn pwa‿yo. Kŭrŏch'i‿man chŏnggŏjang‿ŭn mot‿pwa‿ yo.   *The hotel I see. But I can't see the railroad station.*

In English we usually stress the emphasis the other way: KIM's in the army, but ME, I'm in the air force. This is why some people will tell you this Korean particle shows emphasis rather than de-emphasis:

Kim‿sŏnsaeng‿ŭn yuk-kun ie‿yo. Kŭrŏch'i ‿man, na‿nŭn konggun‿ie‿yo.   *Mr. Kim is (in) the ARMY. But I'm (in) the AIR FORCE.*

When you first mention a subject, you usually use the subject particle. But if you keep on talking about the same thing, you either repeat the subject (in the same or slightly different words) with the topic particle, or you just don't mention it:

Nae ch'in-gu＿ga Miguk ＿sŏ wasse＿yo. (Ch'in-gu＿nŭn) Miguk saram ＿ie＿yo. (Kŭ saram＿ ŭn) kunin＿ŭro Han-guk wasse＿yo. (Kŭ saram＿ ŭn) yukkun changgyo＿ -e＿yo. (Kŭ saram＿ŭn) Sŏul＿e＿sŏ salgo isse＿ yo.	*My friend came from America. He is an American. He came to Korea as a serviceman. He's an army officer. He's living in Seoul.*

The one-shape particle **to** (which sounds like **do** of course after a voiced sound) is a kind of opposite; it has the meaning *too, also, indeed, even*. This particle reinforces the emphasis on the preceding word with reference either to some other part of the sentence or to something outside the sentence:

Kŭ haksaeng＿to chigŭm hakkyo＿sŏ Han-guk＿ mal＿ŭl kongbu hae＿ yo.	*That student is studying Korean in school now too (as well as someone else).* OR *Even that student (to my surprise)......*
Haksaeng＿i chigŭm＿to hakkyo＿sŏ Han-guk＿ mal＿ŭl kongbu hae＿ yo.	*That student is studying Korean in school right at this very moment (unexpected though it be).* OR *......studying now also (as well as at other times).*

(34)

Kŭ haksaeng‿i chigŭm hakkyo‿sŏ‿to Han-guk‿mal‿ŭl kongbu hae‿yo.	*That student is now study-ing Korean at school too (as well as at home or somewhere else).*
Kŭ haksaeng‿i chigŭm hakkyo‿sŏ Han-guk‿ mal‿to kongbu hae‿yo.	*That student is studying Korean at school now too (as well as other subjects).*

Notice that the English words *too* and *also* are ambiguous in reference wherever you put them in the sentence, but the Korean particle **to** always refers to the word preceding it. Notice also that the sub-ject and object particles are not used when you use **to** (just as they are not with the topic particle).

Since the particle **to** reinforces the emphasis, we might expect the phrase with which it occurs to be moved over near the end of the sentence, and this sometimes happens, but it seems to be unnecessary since the particle itself lends all the emphasis needed.

Now notice the translation of the following sen-tences :

Pyŏngjŏng‿to subyŏng‿ to wasse‿yo.	*Both soldiers and sailors came.*
Mul‿to sul‿to mŏgŏsse ‿yo.	*I drank (ate) both water and liquor.*
Ach'im‿e‿to pam‿e‿ to il hae‿yo.	*I work both in the mornings and in the evenings.*
Yŏnp'il‿lo‿to mannyŏn-p'il‿lo‿to ssŏsse‿yo.	*I wrote both with a pencil and with a pen.*
Miguk‿e‿sŏ‿to, Ilbon‿ sŏ‿to‿wasse‿yo.	*They came from both America and Japan.*
Chip‿to pat‿to isse‿yo.	*I have both a house and a garden (field).*

Kim‿sŏnsaeng‿to, Ma‿ sŏnsaeng‿to, Chang‿ sŏnsaeng‿to pwasse‿ yo.	*I saw Mr. Kim, and Mr. Ma, and Mr. Chang, all three.*

When you have **to** after each of two affirmative phrases, the translation is *both ...... and ....* If there are more than two phrases, the translation comes out *and ......, and ......, and ......, all 3 (or 4, or 5).*

Now look at some negative sentences:

Pyŏngjŏng‿to subyŏng‿ to an‿wasse‿yo.	*Neither the soldier nor the sailor came.*
Ach'im‿e‿to pam‿e‿to il haji anhŏ yo.	*I work neither in the morn- ing nor at night.*
Chip‿to pat‿to ŏpse‿ yo.	*I haven't got either a house or a garden.*
Kim‿sŏnsaeng‿to, Ma‿ sŏnsaeng ‿ to, Chang sŏnsaeng‿to, an‿wasse ‿yo.	*Neither Mr. Kim, nor Mr. Ma, nor Mr. Chang, none of them came.*

The translation is *neither ...... nor ......* or *not either ...... or ......*

Lesson 16

NUMERALS

The Koreans have two sets of numerals ; one of these they borrowed from the Chinese. Up to 99, both sets are used — for 100 and above you use only the Chinese set. The numerals above 10 are usually in combinations of the first ten numerals: 11 is 10-1, 12 is 10-2, 20 (in the Chinese system) is 2-10. But there are a number of sound changes involved. Some of the native Korean numerals have two shapes: the shortened shape is used only when the numeral is right in front of the word with which you are counting. For example **hana** means *1* but *1 o'clock* is **han⌣ si** and *1 person* is **han⌣saram**:

MEANING	NATIVE NUMERALS		CHINESE NUMERAL
	(ordinary)	(shortened)	
1	**hana**	**han**	**il**
2	**tul**	**tu**	**i**
3	**set**	**se**	**sam**
4	**net**	**ne**	**sa**
5	**tasŏt**		**o**
6	**yŏsŏt**		**yuk**
7	**ilgop**		**ch'il**
8	**yŏdŏl(p)**		**p'al**
9	**ahop**		**ku**
10	**yŏl**		**sip**
11	**yŏl-hana**	**yŏl-han**	**sip-il**
12	**yŏl-(t)tul**	**yŏl-(t)tu**	**sip-i**
13	**yŏl-(s)set**	**yŏl-(s)se**	**sip-sam**
14	**yŏl-let**	**yŏl-le**	**sip-sa**
15	**yŏl-(t)tasŏt**		**sip-o**
16	**yŏl-yŏsŏt**		**sim-nyuk**
17	**yŏl-ilgop**		**sip-ch'il**
18	**yŏl-yŏdŏl(p)**		**sip-p'al**
19	**yŏl-ahop**		**sip-ku**
20	**sŭmul**		**i-sip**

21	sŭmul hana	sumul han	i-sip il
22	sŭmul (t)tul	sŭmul (t)tu	i-sip i
23	sŭmul (s)set	sŭmul (s)se	i-sip sam
24	sŭmul let	sŭmul le	i-sip sa
25		sŭmul (t)tasot	i-sip o
26		sŭmul yŏsŏt	i-sip yuk
			(i-sim-nyuk)
27		sŭmul ilgop	i-sip ch'il
28		sŭmul yŏdŏl(p)	i-sip p'al
29		sŭmul ahop	i-sip ku
30		sŏl(h)ŭn	sam-sip
40		mahŭn	sa-sip
50		swin	o-sip
60		yesŭn	yuk-sip
70		ilhŭn	ch'il-(s)sip
80		yŏdŭn	p'al-(s)sip
90		ahŭn	ku-sip
100		—	paek ; il-baek
200			i-baek
300			sam-baek
400			sa-baek
500			o-baek
600			yuk-paek
700			ch'il-baek
800			p'al-baek
900			ku-baek
1000			ch'ŏn ; ilch'ŏn
2000			i-ch'ŏn
3000			sam-ch'ŏn
4000			sa-ch'ŏn
5000			o-ch'ŏn
6000			yuk-ch'on
7000			ch'il-ch'ŏn
8000			p'al-ch'ŏn
9000			ku-ch'ŏn

10,000	man ; il-man
20,000	i-man
30,000	sam-man
100,000	sim-man
1,000,000	paeng-man

Lesson 17

NOUNS ENDING IN -t

In Lesson 3, we learned that only the consonants
p, **t**, **k**, **m**, **n**, **ng**, and **l** occur before a pause or
another consonant. But some words have basic forms
that end in other sounds, and these have to change
before pause or a consonant. When you hear a noun
ending in **t** you are not sure whether the basic form
of the noun ends in **t**, **s**, **ch**, **ch'**, or **t'**.

As it happens, nearly all these nouns have basic
forms that end in **s**, so we can consider the others
as individual exceptions and make a rule : a noun
which you hear with a final **t**, has a final **s** when it
is linked with a particle beginning with a vowel, or
when it is linked with the verb **ie‿yo** 'is'. Here
are some examples :

MEANING	NOUN	PARTICLE	ie‿yo
thing	kŏt	kŏs‿i	kŏs‿ie‿yo
place	kot	kos‿e	kos‿ie‿yo
what ?	muŏt ?	muŏs‿i ?	muŏs‿ie‿yo ?
clothes	ot	os‿ŭn	os‿ie‿yo

(39)

three	**set**	ses＿i	ses＿ie＿yo
four	**net**	nes＿ŭl	nes＿ie＿yo
five	**tasŏt**	tasŏs＿ŭn	tasŏs＿ie＿yo
six	**yŏsŏt**	yŏsŏs＿i	yŏsŏs＿ie＿yo

The individual exceptions are regularized by many Koreans so that you may hear both forms:

flower	**kkot**	{ kkoch'＿i { kkos＿i	kkoch'＿ie＿yo kkos＿ie＿yo
how many?	**met?**	{ mech'＿ina? { mes＿ina?	mech'＿ie＿yo? mes＿ie＿yo?
daytime	**nat**	{ nach＿e { nas＿e	nach＿ie＿yo nas＿ie＿yo
dry field	**pat**	{ pat'＿e { pas＿e	pat'＿ie＿yo pas＿ie＿yo

Lesson 18

COUNTING THINGS

In English we can say either *2 steers* or *2 head of cattle*. In the same way, Koreans say either **so tul** *2 cows* or **so tu mari** *2 head of cattle*. But expressions like *2* HEAD *of cattle*, *4* SHEETS *of paper*, *a* CONTAINER *of milk*, *3* PIECES *of candy*, *6* ITEMS *of laundry* are much more common in Korean. The words in capital letters can be called CLASSIFIERS—they tell you something about the shape or looks of the thing you're counting. Or sometimes they tell you the unit by which you are measuring the thing: *3* CUPS

of sugar, 2 TABLESPOONFULS *of sugar,* 1 POUND *of sugar.*
Most Korean classifiers are used with the native set
of numerals, but a few common ones are used with
the Chinese set. Here are some useful classifiers:

USED WITH KOREAN NUMERALS

si	*o'clock*	mari	*animals, fish*
sigan	*hours*	pǒn	*times*
*tal	*months*	*chang	*flat objects, news-papers*
sal	*years old*	*chan	*cupfuls*
saram	*people*	ch'ae	*buildings*
pun	*honored people*	tae	*vehicles, machines*
kwǒn	*bound volumes*	kae	*items, units, objects*

The starred items count 3 and 4 with the special
shapes sǒk and nǒk instead of se and ne:

sǒk tal	*3 months*	nǒk chang	*4 flat objects.*

USED WITH CHINESE NUMERALS

pun	*minutes*	Wǒn	*Won, Yen (money)*
(n)yǒn	*years*	Hwan	*Hwan (money)*
ch'ǔng	*floor (of build-ings)*	Chǒn	*Chon, Sen, & Cents*
(l)i, (n)i	*miles, Li*		

Notice that i‿pun means 2 *minutes* but tu‿pun
means 2 *honored persons.*

When you are using a noun, a particle and a number expression (a numeral+a classifier, or a numeral
all by itself), there are three possible ways to phrase
your sentence, and all are common:

> Tu ch'aek‿i isse‿yo.
> Ch'aek tul‿i isse‿yo.
> Ch'aek‿i tul isse yo.

(41)

These all mean *I have 2 books*. You can say the same thing with a classifier :

Tu_kwŏn ch'aek_i isse_yo. Ch'aek tu_kwŏn_i isse_yo. Ch'aek_i tu_kwŏn isse_yo.

Here are some examples of number expressions in sentences :

Sinmun_ŭl tu_chang sasse_yo.	*I bought 2 newspapers.*
Ach'im_mada sinmun _ŭl met_chang sa_ yo ?	*How many newspapers do you buy each morning ?*
Chadongch'a han_tae_ man isse_yo.	*We have only one automobile.*
Ton_i il_tchŏn_to ŏpse_yo.	*I haven't a cent.*
Chungguk pyŏngjŏng se _saram ŭl pwasse_ yo.	*I saw 3 Chinese-soldiers.*
I ch'aek_ŭl tu_pŏn ilgŏsse_yo.	*I read this book twice.*
Kŭ yŏnghwa_rŭl se_ pŏn pwasse_yo.	*I saw that movie 3 times.*
Chŏmwon_hant'e (Han- guk ton_ŭl) i-ch'ŏn Hwan chuŏsse_yo.	*I gave the clerk 2000 Hwan (of Korean money).*
I chip_i met_ch'ŭng isse_yo ?	*How many stories does this building have ?*
Os_ŭl i_ch'ŭng_e_sŏ p'arŏ_yo.	*They sell clothes on the 2nd floor.*
Na_nŭn pŏlssŏ sam_ nyŏn_(t)tongan Han- guk_e isse_yo.	*I am (=have been) in Korea already 3 years (long).*
Il_lyŏn_hu_e Miguk _e tora ka_yo.	*I go back (return) to America after a year.*

(42)

l_nyŏn_chŏn_e Pusan _e salgo issŏssŏ_yo.	*Two years ago (before) I was living in Pusan.*
Ttal_i met_sal_ie_ yo ?	*How old is your daughter ?*
Yŏl-yŏdŏl (s)sal_ie_yo.	*She's 18.*
Na_nŭn mahŭn_sal_ ie_yo.	*I'm 40.*
An(h)ae_nŭn sŏl(h)ŭn ahop_sal_ie_yo.	*My wife is 39.*

Lesson 19

TELLING TIME

To say what time it is, you use the Korean numer-als followed by **si** *o'clock* :

han_si	*1 o'clock*
tu_si	*2 o'clock*

To say *half-past* you add the word **pan** *and a half* at the end of the expression :

tu_si pan	*2 : 30*

To say *and so-many minutes* you use the Chinese numerals and the noun **pun** *minutes* :

se_si sip_pun	*3 : 15*

If you want to specify a.m. and p.m. you put the words **ojŏn** *forenoon* and **ohu** *afternoon* in front of the time expression :

ojŏn ahop‿si pan	9 : 30 a.m.
ohu ne‿si sa-sip‿pun	4 : 40 p.m.

To say *so-and-so-many* HOURS you use the Korean numerals and the noun **sigan** *hour* :

Yŏl‿(s)sigan kŏllyŏ‿yo.	It takes 10 hours.
Tu‿sigan‿i isse‿yo.	We have 2 hours.

Here are some examples of time expressions in sentences :

Met‿si‿-e‿yo ?	What time is it ?
Han‿si‿-e‿yo.	It's 1 o'clock.
Han‿si pan‿ie‿yo.	It's 1 : 30.
Tu‿si sip‿pun‿ie‿yo.	It's 2 : 10
Tasŏt‿si o‿pun‿ie‿yo.	It's 5 : 50.
Ohu ne‿si sip-o‿pun‿ ie‿yo.	It's 4 : 15 p.m.
Ojŏn ahop‿si pan‿e sijak hae‿yo.	We begin at 9 : 30 a.m.
Ach'im yŏdŏl‿(s)si‿ puthŏ pam yŏl‿(s)si ‿kkaji punju hae‿ yo.	I'm busy from 8 in the morning till 10 at night.

Lesson 20

DAYS AND WEEKS

Counting days is somewhat irregular. Up to 20, the following system is most common, both for counting the days and for giving the day of the month.

How many days?	
What day of the month?	mech'‿il ?
1(st)	haru, haro
2(nd)	it'ŭl
3(nd)	sahŭl
4(th)	nahŭl
5(th)	tassae
6(th)	yŏssae
7(th)	ire
8(th)	yŏdŭre
9(th)	ahŭre
10(th)	yŏlhŭl
11(th)	yŏl‿haru
12(th)	yŏl‿it'ŭl
13(th)	yŏl‿(s)sahŭl
14(th)	yŏl‿lahŭl
15(th)	yŏl‿(t)tassae
16(th)	yŏl‿yŏssae
17(th)	yŏl‿ire
18(th)	yŏl‿yŏdŭre
19(th)	yŏl‿ahŭre
20(th)	sŭmu‿nal

But alongside this system, there is also a Chinese system using the classifier **il** *day* and the regular Chinese numerals : **il‿il, i‿il, sam‿il, sa‿il, o‿il,** etc.

Below 20, this is used only for dates, and is more formal than the other way of saying the days : **yuk‿ il** *the 6th day of the month.*

Above 20, this system is the only one used : **i-sip‿ il‿il** *21 days* OR *the 21st day of the month;* **i-sip‿ i‿il** *22 days* OR *the 22nd day of the month;* **sam-sip‿sam‿il** *33 days.*

The names of the days of the week are as follows:

What day of the week?	Musŭn yoil?
Monday	Wŏl-yoil (wŏ-ryo-il)
Tuesday	Hwa-yoil
Wednesday	Su-yoil
Thursday	Mok-yoil (mo-gyo-il)
Friday	Kŭm-yoil (Kŭ-myo-il)
Saturday	T'o-yoil
Sunday	Il-yoil (i-ryo-il)

Weeks are counted with either the Korean or the Chinese numerals and for a classifier you can use either **chuil** or **chugan**—both mean *week*:

How many weeks?	Met‿chugan?
1 week	han‿chuil, il‿(t)chuil, han‿chugan, il‿(t)chugan
2 weeks	tu‿chuil, i‿chuil, tu‿chugan, i‿chugan
3 weeks	se‿chuil, sam‿chuil, se‿chugan, sam‿chugan

Lesson 21

MONTHS AND YEARS

Months are *COUNTED* with the classifier **tal** and the Korean numerals: Met‿tal, han‿tal, tu‿tal, sŏk‿tal, nŏk‿tal, tasŏt‿tal *How many, 1, 2, 3, 4, 5 months;* or with the classifier **kae-wŏl** and the Chinese numerals: **il‿(k)kae-wŏl, i‿kae-wŏl, sam‿kae-wŏl, sa‿kae-wŏl, o‿kae-wŏl.**

Months are NAMED with combinations of the Chinese numerals and -wŏl *month*, but there are a few irregularities, starred in the list below. Notice that January has two names:

January	**Il-wŏl**	(sounds like (**i-rwŏl**))
	Chŏngwŏl	
February	**I-wŏl**	
March	**Sam-wŏl**	
April	**Sa-wŏl**	
May	**O-wŏl**	
June	***Yu-wŏl**	
July	**Ch'il-wŏl**	(sounds like **ch'i-rwŏl**)
August	**P'al-wŏl**	(sounds like **p'a-rwŏl**)
September	**Ku-wŏl**	
October	***Si-wŏl**	
November	**Sip-il-wŏl**	(sounds like **si-bi-rwŏl**)
December	**Sip-i-wŏl**	(sounds like **si-bi-wŏl**)

The seasons are **pom** *spring*, **yŏrŭm** *summer*, **kaŭl** *autumn*, and **kyŏul** *winter*.

Years are counted or named by using the Chinese numerals and the classifier **(n)yŏn**, and there are a few sound changes:

il‿lyŏn, i‿nyŏn, sam‿nyŏn, sa‿nyŏn, o‿nyŏn, yung‿nyŏn, ch'il‿lyŏn, p'al‿lyŏn, ku‿nyŏn, sim‿nyŏn.

Note also **paeng‿nyŏn** *100 years*, **ch'ŏn‿nyŏn** *1000 years*.

Dates are given like this: **Ch'ŏn ku-baek o-sip sa‿ nyŏn, Sip-i-wŏl sip-o‿il.** *15 December 1954.* If you want to add the day of the week and the time:

Chŏngwŏl ku‿il, T'oyoil, ohu se‿si sip-o‿pun.
3 : 15 p.m., Saturday, 9 January 1954.

Lesson 22

NEGATIVE SENTENCES

You have learned to say *no* with **Ani** or **Ani‿yo**.
To make a complete negative sentence, you can use
an abbreviated form of this word (**an**) in front of the
verb :

Sinmun‿ŭl an sasse‿ yo.	*I didn't buy a newspaper.*
Kim‿sŏnsaeng‿i an wa‿yo.	*Mr. Kim isn't coming.*
Chungguk pyŏngjŏng‿ ŭl an pwasse‿yo.	*I didn't see any Chinese soldiers.*

But you *do not* use **an** with **isse‿yo**; there is a
special verb **ŏpse‿yo** *does not exist.*

You can make a stronger negative by using **mot**
not at all; not possibly; can't instead of **an** :

Sinmun‿ŭl mot sasse‿ yo.	*I didn't buy a newspaper at all; I couldn't buy a news-paper.*
Kim sŏnsaeng‿i mot wa‿yo.	*Mr. Kim can't come; Mr. Kim isn't coming at all.*
Chungguk pyŏngjŏng‿ ŭl mot pwasse‿yo.	*I couldn't see any Chinese soldiers; I saw no Chinese soldiers at all.*

Except for very short sentences, Koreans prefer to

say their negatives in a more complicated way. They change the verb to a special form we'll call the -CHI form (it often sounds like -JI of course) and then add some form of either **an hae‿yo** *doesn't do* or **mot hae‿yo** *can't possibly do*.

Sinmun‿ŭl saji { **an haesse‿yo.**
{ **mot haesse‿yo.**

Kim‿sŏnsaeng‿i oji { **an hae‿yo.**
{ **mot hae‿yo.**

Chungguk pyŏngjŏng‿ŭl poji { **an haesse‿yo.**
{ **mot haesse‿yo.**

A further complication: Koreans often substitute the verb **anhŏ‿yo** for **an hae‿yo.** (This **anhŏ‿yo** was originally just a contraction of **an hae‿yo.**)

Sinmun‿ŭl saji anhŏsse‿yo.
Kim‿sŏnsaeng‿i oji anhŏ‿yo.
Chungguk pyŏngjŏng‿ŭl poji anhŏsse‿yo.

Here are some examples of negative sentences:

Na‿nŭn hakkyo‿e‿sŏ kongbu haji anhŏ‿yo.	*I'm not studying in school.*
Na‿nŭn ton‿i ŏpse‿yo. Kŭrae‿sŏ, yŏnghwagwan‿e kaji mot hae‿yo.	*I haven't any money; so I can't go to the theater.*
Kŭ‿yŏnghwa‿rŭl mot pwasse‿yo.	*I couldn't see that movie.*
Anhae‿ga onŭl‿ach'im sinmun‿ŭl poji anhŏsse‿yo.	*My wife didn't read the newspaper this morning.*
Sangjŏm‿e kasse‿yo. Kŭrŏch'i‿man, kudu‿rŭl mot sasse‿yo.	*I went to the store. But I couldn't buy any shoes.*

Kŏgi‿sŏ kudu‿rŭl p'alji anhŏ‿yo?	*Don't they sell shoes there?*
Mot p'arŏ‿yo.	*They don't sell them at all.*
Kŭ tu pyŏngjŏng‿i Yŏngŏ‿ro mot haesse‿yo.	*Those 2 soldiers couldn't (didn't) speak in English.*
Na‿nŭn Han-guk‿mal‿ŭl chal mot hae‿yo.	*I can't speak Korean well.*

You will learn to make the **-chi** forms for new verbs in Lesson 24.

The negative of an equational sentence like $A=B$ is a bit different:

English formula	*Korean formula*
$\left.\begin{array}{l} A = B \\ A \ is \ B \end{array}\right\}$	**A‿ga, B‿-e‿yo**

Examples:

Nae‿ga moksa‿-e‿yo.	*I'm a preacher.*
Kim‿sŏnsaeng‿i pyŏngjŏng‿ie yo.	*Mr. Kim is a soldier.*

English formula	*Korean formula*
$\left.\begin{array}{l} A \ does \ not = B \\ A \ is \ not \ B \end{array}\right\}$	**A‿ga, B‿ga ani‿-e‿yo**

Nae‿ga pyŏngjŏng‿i ani‿-e‿yo.
Kim‿sŏnsaeng‿i moksa‿ga ani‿-e‿yo.

Notice that the affirmative sentence attaches the verb **ie‿yo** directly to the noun (B) but in the negative sentence the word **ani** is attached to the copula and the noun (B) is followed by the subject particle. The noun A is also followed by the subject particle.

(It is the bigger subject of the whole expression **B⌣ ga⌣ani-e yo.**) But this can be changed to the topic particle in order to emphasize the *not*.

Lesson 23

WHERE THINGS ARE

To locate objects in English you usually need only a preposition *in, at, on, under, behind*, but sometimes you use a prepositional phrase which includes a noun *in front of, on top of, at the side of*. This is the usual Korean way of doing it. Here are some of these 'place words' which are nouns in Korean. To locate a thing or an event, you use the particle **e** *at, in*, etc. or **(e)⌣sŏ** *happens at* after one of these words:

an	*inside* (something spacious)	**ap'**	*front*
sok	*inside* (something small or rather full)	**twi**	*behind*
		yŏp'	*beside*
		oen p'yŏn	*left side of*
pakk	*outside*	**parŭn p'yŏn**	*right side of*
u, wi	(on) *top of, above*	**majŭn p'yŏn**	*across from*
arae	*below, underneath*	**ta(ŭ)m**	*next* (to)
mit'	(at the) *bottom of*	**sai**	*between*

Here are some examples :

Chumŏni sok⌣e muŏs⌣ i isse⌣yo ?	*What do you have in your pocket ?*
Taŭm⌣(p)pang an⌣e⌣ sŏ, muŏs⌣ ŭl hae⌣yo ?	*What are they doing in the next room ?*

Kim_sŏnsaeng yŏp'_e nu_ga anjŏ_yo?	Who sits next to Mr. Kim?
Yebaedang taŭm_e kongwŏn_i isse_yo.	There's a park next to the church.
Chang pakk_e namu_ga poe_yo.	Outside the window a tree can be seen.
Namu mit'_e kae han_mari_ga nuwŏ isse_yo.	A dog is lying at the foot of the tree.
Namu wi_e chip han_chae isse_yo. Ch'am chŏgŏ_yo.	There is a house on top of the tree. It's real small.
Kŭ chip an_e sae_ga salgo isse_yo. Sae chip_ie_yo.	There are birds living in that house. It's a bird house.
Hakkyo oen p'yŏn_e kil_i isse_yo.	There's a road on the right of the school.
Kil majŭn p'yŏn_(ŭi) pat'_e_sŏ_nŭn nongbu_ga il hae_yo.	In the field on the other side of the road a farmer is working.
Pat twi_e chip_i isse_yo. Nongbu_ŭi chip_ie_yo.	There's a house behind the field. It's the farmer's house.
Chip ap'_e_sŏ nongbu puin_i il hae_yo.	In front of the house the farmer's wife is working.
Na_nŭn yŏnp'il_ŭl ŏdi nohasse_yo?	Where did I put my pencil?
Kabang sok_e nohasse yo?	Did I put it in my briefcase?
Chumŏni sok_e nohasse _yo?	Did I put it in my pocket?
Pot'ong ch'aek-sang u_e noha_yo.	Usually I put it on the desk.
Ch'aek-sang arae_(e) ŏpse_yo?	Isn't it under the desk?
Maru u_e ŏpse_yo?	Isn't it on the floor?

Kǔ tu ch'aek sai‿(e) isse‿yo ? *Is it between those two books ?*

Kǔrǒssǔmnida. I ch'aek ‿hago kǔ ch'aek sai ‿e isse‿yo. *You're right. It's between this book and that one.*

Na‿nǔn yǒnp'il‿ǔl kǔ ch'aek‿kwa i ch'aek sai‿e nohasse‿yo. *I put my pencil between that book and this one.*

Lesson 24

VERBS AND ADJECTIVES

The nucleus of a Korean sentence is the verb expression at the end. A verb in Korean is a word which means either *something happens*, *someone* DOES *something* or *something* IS *a certain way*.

Most English adjectives correspond to verbs in Korean : **k'ŏ‿yo** *is big*, **chǒgǒ‿yo** *is little*, **manhǒ‿ yo** *is much! are many*, **ippǒ‿yo** *is cute* etc. Notice that these Korean words do not mean *big*, *little*, *much, cute* but IS *big*, IS *little*, IS *much*, IS *cute*.

Later you will learn how to put such verbs in front of nouns to modify them — in Korean instead of saying *a big house* you have to say the equivalent of *a house which is big*.

Now there are a few English adjectives which correspond to Korean nouns : **sae** *new*, **on** *whole*, *entire*. These can modify a following noun just by being in front of it: **sae moja** *new hat,* **on sege** *whole world.* But most English adjectives correspond to Korean verbs.

Each Korean verb appears in a great many different forms—as many as 500. Some of these forms are fairly rare, but many are common. In this book, you will learn a few of the most useful forms and find out a little about the structure of verb forms in general, so that you will be better prepared to cope with the bewildering number of forms you hear.

Each verb form consists of a BASE and an ENDING. Sometimes the ending can be divided into several parts, but we will talk about each ending as a unit. There are two things to learn about each verb base: (1) how it is used, what it means; (2) how its shape changes when you add the various endings. And there are two things to learn about each ending: (A) how it is used, what it means; (B) how its shape changes when you attach it to the various kinds of bases.

Fortunately the shape changes are rather systematic, and if you learn a few typical verbs you can make up forms for new verbs by analogy.

The most complicated rules are for the INFINITIVE or -ŏ ending. Since this is the form which occurs with the particle **yo** in the polite style, it is perhaps best just to memorize the verb from this form to start with and find one other form where the base of the verb appears in its basic form. (The shape changes we are considering here are different from the automatic sound changes by which **ch** sounds like **j**, **k** sounds like **g**, **t** sounds like **d**, **b** sounds like **p**, and **l** sounds like **r** in certain surroundings. These automatic sound changes we will omit as being self-explanatory.)

Below you will find a list of typical verb bases, showing (1) the polite present form (-ŏ **yo**, -**a yo**, -**e yo**, with some irregularities); (2) the polite past form (-ŏsse **yo** or -**asse yo** with some irregularities); (3) the polite present negative (-**chi anhŏ yo**). To make the negative past you replace **anhŏ yo** with **anhŏsse yo**:

chapchi anhŏsse yo   *didn't catch*

Finally there is given the basic shape of the BASE, from which the various forms are predictable. There are two general classes of bases: CONSONANT and VOWEL. The basic shape of consonant bases is found when you remove the -ŏ **yo** ending; the basic shape of vowel verbs appears when you take away the -**chi** ending.

I. CONSONANT BASES

MEANING	Does; Is	Did; Was	Doesn't; Isn't	BASE
catches	chabŏ yo	chabŏsse yo	chapchi anhŏ yo	chab-
is high	nop'a yo	nop'asse yo	nopchi anhŏ yo	nop'-
is non-existent	ŏpse yo	ŏpsŏsse yo	—	ŏps-
closes	tadŏ yo	tadŏsse yo	tatchi anhŏ yo	tad-

is like	kat'e yo	kat'ŏsse yo	katchi anhŏ yo	kat'-
laughs	usŏ yo	usŏsse yo	utchi anhŏ yo	us-
exists	isse yo	issŏsse yo	—	iss-
finds	ch'ajŏ yo	ch'ajŏsse yo	chatchi anhŏ yo	ch'aj-
washes	ssich'ŏ yo	ssich'ŏsse yo	ssitchi anhŏ yo	ssich'-
reads	ilgŏ yo	ilgŏsse yo	ikchi anhŏ yo	ilg-
loses	ilhŏ yo	ilhŏsse yo	ilch'i anhŏ yo	ilh-
licks	halt'ŏ yo	halt'ŏsse yo	haltchi anhŏ yo	halt'-
steps on	palbŏ yo	palbŏsse yo	paltchi anhŏ yo	palb-
chants	ŭlp'ŏ yo	ŭlp'ŏsse yo	ŭltchi anhŏ yo	ŭlp'-
puts	noha yo	nohasse yo	noch'i anhŏ yo	noh-
eats	mŏgŏ yo	mŏgŏsse yo	mŏkchi anhŏ yo	mŏg-
cuts	kkakkŏ yo	kkakkŏsse yo	kkakchi anhŏ yo	kkakk-
shampoos	kamŏ yo	kamŏsse yo	kamtchi anhŏ yo	kam-
is young	chŏlmŏ yo	chŏlmŏsse yo	chŏmtchi anhŏ yo	chŏlm-
wears on feet	sinŏ yo	sinŏsse yo	sintchi anhŏ yo	sin-
sits	anjŏ yo	anjŏsse yo	antchi anhŏ yo	anj-
breaks	kkŭnhŏ yo	kkŭnhŏsse yo	kkunch'i anhŏ yo	kkŭnh-

II. VOWEL BASES

MEANING	*Does; Is*	*Did; Was*	*Doesn't; Isn't*	BASE
is, equals	{ ie yo	iŏsse yo	—	(i)-
	-e yo	-yŏsse yo	—	—
rests	swiŏ yo	swiŏsse yo	swiji anhŏ yo	swi-
waits	kidaryŏ yo	kidaryŏsse yo	kidariji anhŏ yo	kidari-
counts	se yo	sesse yo	seji anhŏ yo	se-
becomes	toe yo	toesse yo	toeji anhŏ yo	toe-
pays	nae yo	naesse yo	naeji anhŏ yo	nae-
writes	ssŏ yo	ssŏsse yo	ssŭji anhŏ yo	ssŭ-
goes	ka yo	kasse yo	kaji anhŏ yo	ka-
gives	chuŏ yo	chuŏsse yo	chuji anhŏ yo	chu-
sees, reads	pwa yo	pwasse yo	poji anhŏ yo	po-

(VOWEL BASES WITH IRREGULAR FORMS)

does	hae yo	haesse yo	haji anhŏ yo	ha-
calls	pullŏ yo	pullŏsse yo	purŭji anhŏ yo	purŭ-
is blue, green	p'urŭrŏ yo	p'urŭrŏsse yo	p'urŭji anhŏ yo	p'urŭ-

NOTE: The -chi forms for isse yo, ŏpse yo, and ie yo are itchi, ŏpchi, and iji. They are not used in the negative construction.

Most of the other verbs you have met will fit into

(57)

one of the above categories. For example, **wa yo** *comes* works just like **pwa yo** *sees*:

wa yo,   **wasse yo,**   **oji anhŏ yo,**   **o-.**

Ippŏ yo *is cute* and **k'ŏ** yo *is big* are like **ssŏ yo** *writes*:

ippŏ yo,	**ippŏsse yo,**	**ippŭji anhŏ yo,**	**ippŭ-**
k'ŏ yo,	**k'ŏsse yo,**	**k'ŭji anhŏ yo,**	**k'ŭ-**

Chŏgŏ yo *is small* works like **mŏgŏ yo** *eats*. **Manhŏ yo** *is much, are many* and **anhŏ yo** *does not, is not* have forms like those of **kkŭnhŏ yo** *cuts*; **padŏ yo** *gets* has forms like those of **tadŏ yo** *closes*. **Molla yo** *does not know* and **mallŏ yo** *gets dry* works like **pullŏ yo** *calls*:

mallŏsse yo,   **marŭji anhŏ yo,**   **marŭ-**

Here are a few examples of these verbs in sentences.

Kŭ san i nop'a yo.	*That mountain is tall.*
Wae mun ŭl tatchi anhŏsse yo?	*Why didn't you close the door?*
Kŭ pyŏngjŏng i nae ch'in-gu wa katchi anhŏsse yo.	*That soldier was not like my friend.*
Ŏdi sŏ kŭ ton ŭl ch'ajŏsse yo?	*Where did you find the money?*
Aegi ga wae utchi anhŏ yo?	*Why isn't the baby laughing?*
Moja rŭl ilhŏsse yo.	*I lost my hat.*
Oet'u nŭn ilch'i anhŏsse yo.	*I didn't lose my overcoat.*
Kabang ŭl sang u e noch'i anhŏsse yo.	*I didn't put my briefcase on the table.*

Kǔ saram i kogi rǔl mǒkchi mot hae yo.	*He doesn't eat meat (at all).*
Namp'yǒn i chǒmtchi anhǒ yo.	*My husband isn't young.*
Kǔ saekssi ga sae kudu rǔl sinǒsse yo.	*That girl put on her new shoes.*
Na nǔn (tangsin hant'e) ton ǔl chuji anhǒsse yo.	*I didn't give you any money.*
Ton i ǒpse yo. Kǔrae sǒ, naeji mot hae yo.	*I haven't any money; so, I can't pay (you).*

Lesson 25

RELATIVES

The Korean terms for relatives can be divided into two groups : those for which some of the words differ according to the sex of the person related (whether we're talking about a man's brother or a woman's brother), and those for which the words are the same regardless of the sex of the person related. In the lists some words are given in capital letters ; these are HONORIFIC—they are used about someone else's relatives when you what to show special politeness, or they are used in addressing older relatives of your own :

1.

RELATIVE	MAN'S	WOMAN'S
older brother	ŏnni, HYŎNG (NIM)	oppa, ORABŎ (NIM)
older sister	nuna, NU NIM	ŏnni, HYŎNG (NIM)
younger brother	tongsaeng, au	nam-dongsaeng
younger sister	yŏ-dongsaeng	tongsaeng
brothers	hyŏngje	oppa wa nam-dong-saeng
sisters	chamae	chamae
spouse	an(h)ae, PUIN	namp'yŏn
father-in-law	changin	si-abŏji, SI-ABŎ NIM
mother-in-law	changmo	si-ŏmŏni, SI-ŎMŎ NIM

2.

RELATIVE	ANYBODY'S
grandfather	harabŏji, HARABŎ NIM
grandmother	halmŏni, HALMŎ NIM
parents	pumo, PUMO NIM
father	abŏji, ABŎ NIM
mother	ŏmŏni, ŎMŎ NIM
children	ai(tŭl), ae (tŭl)
son	adŭl, ADŬ NIM
daughter	ttal, TTA NIM
grandchildren	sonju, sonju ai (tŭl)
grandson	sonja
granddaughter	sonnyŏ
son-in-law	sawi
daughter-in-law	menuri, myŏnuri
fiance(e)	yakhonja
cousin	sach'un
uncle	ajŏssi
aunt	ajumŏni
nephew or niece	chok'a
niece	chok'a ttal
nephew	chok'a adŭl
family	kajok, chip, TAEK
members of family	sikku

(60)

NOTE: The words for *grandfather* and *grand-mother* are also used to mean *old man* and *old woman*. The words for *uncle* and *aunt* are used to mean *(older) man*, *(older) lady* especially in expressions by and to children like: ' *The man who lives next door to us ...... Say hello to the lady, dear.*'
Here are some examples of these words in sentences.

Uri chip i k'ŏ yo. Sikku ga manhŏ yo.	*My (our) family's large; there are a lot of us.*
Met pun ie yo?	*How many (honored persons) are you?*
Yŏl han saram ie yo. Na hago anhae hago tul ie yo. Ttal tul isse yo. Adŭl i ses ie yo.	*There are eleven. My wife and I are two. We have two daughters. We have three sons.*
Abŏji hago ŏmŏni ga uri hago salgo isse yo.	*Father and mother are living with us.*
Pumo hago kach'i, ahop saram ie yo.	*Together with my parents that is nine.*
Tto tu pun i ŏpse yo?	*Aren't there still two people (more)?*
Nugu nugu -e yo?	*Who (and who) are they?*
Kwaengi han mari hago kae han mari -e yo.	*They are our cat and dog.*
Ajŏssi ga kwaengi rŭl ttal hant'e chuŏsse yo.	*Uncle gave the cat to my daughter.*
Taŭm chip harabŏji ga kae rŭl uri chip hant'e chuŏsse yo.	*The old man next door gave the dog to our family.*

Lesson 26

HONORIFICS

When you talk about someone who has a relatively
high social status—a government official, a foreign
guest, a minister, a teacher—you use some special
forms called HONORIFICS. These forms are also frequently used of the second person—it's often a way
to show I'm talking about YOU without actually using
a pronoun.

You have come across some honorific nouns already:

pun	*an honored person,*
abŏ nim	*honored father (or father of an honored person)*
taek	*honored house or family*
chinji	*honored food.*

We even find an honorific particle **kke** *to or for (an
honored person)* — this is the honorific equivalent of
hant'e, ege, and **pogo**:

Harabŏ nim kke p'yŏn-ji rŭl ssŏsse yo.	*I wrote a letter to Grandfather.*

Kke sŏ means *from an honored person*:

Moksa nim kke sŏ p'yŏnji rŭl padŏsse yo.	*I received a letter from the pastor.*

(62)

There are also a few special honorific verbs. For *an honored person eats* instead of **mŏgŏ yo** you use **chapsuse yo** or **chapsuŏ yo**. For *an honored person stays or is in a place* you use **kese yo** instead of **isse yo**:

> **Abŏ nim i taek e kese**   *Is your father at home?*
> **yo?**

But for the meaning *an honored person has something* you use **issŭse yo**, the expected honorific of **isse yo**:

> **Abŏ nim i kŭ chapchi**   *Does your father have that*
> **ga issŭse yo?**   *magazine?*

The negative of **kese yo** is an **kese yo**:

> **Chapchi ga ŏpsŭse yo?**   *Doesn't he have it?*
> **Taek e an kese yo?**   *Isn't he home?*

Most verbs are made honorific very easily — you just slip a suffix onto the base before you attach the endings. This suffix has the basic shape **-ŭsi-** after a consonant base, **-si-** after a vowel base. But the final **i** drops when the ending begins with a vowel. Here are some examples with verbs you have had:

MEANING	ORDINARY		HONORIFIC	
	PRESENT	PAST	PRESENT	PAST
catches	chabŏ yo	chabŏsse yo	chabŭse yo	chabŭsŏsse yo
closes	tadŏ yo	tadŏsse yo	tadŭse yo	tadŭsŏsse yo
laughs	usŏ yo	usŏsse yo	usŭse yo	usŭsŏsse yo
reads	ilgŏ yo	ilgŏsse yo	ilgŭse yo	ilgŭsŏsse yo

MEANING	ORDINARY		HONORIFIC	
	PRESENT	PAST	PRESENT	PAST
puts	noha yo	nohasse yo	nohŭse yo	nohŭsŏsse yo
cuts	kkakkŏ yo	kkakkŏsse yo	kkakkŭse yo	kkakkŭsŏsse yo
sits	anjŏ yo	anjŏsse yo	anjŭse yo	anjŭsŏsse yo
rests	swiŏ yo	swiŏsse yo	swise yo	swisŏsse yo
pays	nae yo	naesse yo	naese yo	naesŏsse yo
writes	ssŏ yo	ssŏsse yo	ssŭse yo	ssŭsŏsse yo
goes	ka yo	kasse yo	kase yo	kasŏsse yo
gives	chuŏ yo	chuŏsse yo	chuse yo	chusŏsse yo
sees *reads*	pwa yo	pwasse yo	pose yo	posŏsse yo
does	hae yo	haesse yo	hase yo	hasŏsse yo

For negative honorific statements, you can make either the -chi form or the anhŏ yo honorific; or if you really want to do it up fancy, make both of them honorific: chusiji anhŏ yo, chuji anhŭse yo, chusiji anhŭse yo; chusiji anhŏsse yo, chuji anhŭsŏsse yo, chusiji anhŭsŏsse yo.

In addition to the verb chuŏ yo *gives* there is another verb tŭryŏ yo *gives to someone honored*. So chuse yo means *someone honored gives* or *you give me*, tŭryŏ yo means *I give someone honored* or *I give you*, and tŭlise yo means *someone honored gives someone honored* or *you give someone honored*.

When you command someone to do something, it's good to use the honorific form of the verb:

Iri ose yo!	*Come here!*
Chuse yo!	*Give (it to me)!*

Notice how the use of honorifics makes a conversation between YOU and ME quite clear even though we don't use pronouns:

Ŏdi kase yo?	*Where are you going?*
Up'yŏn-guk e ka yo.	*I'm going to the post office.*
Ŏdi sŏ osŏsse yo?	*Where did you come from?*
Chip e sŏ wasse yo.	*I came from home.*
Chinji chapsusŏsse yo?	*Have you eaten?*
Ajik an mŏgŏsse yo.	*I haven't eaten yet.*
Kim Poktong abŏ nim ise yo?	*Are you Kim Poktong's father?*
Ani yo. Kim Haksu abŏji -e yo.	*No, I'm Kim Haksu's father.*
Muŏs ŭl hase yo?	*What do you do?*
Nongbu -se yo?	*Are you a farmer?*
Ani yo. Nongbu ga ani -e yo. Chikkong ie yo.	*No, I'm not a farmer. I'm a factory worker.*
Kongjang e sŏ il hae yo.	*I work at a factory.*
Myŏngham i issŭse yo?	*Do you have a name-card?*
Pŏlssŏ tŭliji anhŏsse yo?	*Didn't I already give it to you?*
Kabang ŭl ŏdi nohasse yo?	*Where did I put the brief-case?*
Kabang ŭl ŏdi nohŭsŏsse yo?	*Where did you put the brief-case?*

Lesson 27

" BUT "

You have learned the expression **Kurŏch'i man** *But*:

Sangjŏm e ka yo. Kŭrŏch'i man kudu rŭl an sa yo.	*I go to the store. But I don't buy any shoes.*

If you want to link two such sentences together more closely, you can change the verb of the first to the **-chi** form and add the particle **man**:

Sangjŏm e kaji man, kudu rŭl an sa yo.	*I go to the store, but I don't buy any shoes.*

If the verb is in the past, you have to use the past **-chi** form which ends in **-ŏtchi** or **-atchi** (with some irregularities, just like the polite past **-ŏsse yo** and **-asse yo**): Sangjŏm e kasse yo. Kurŏch'i man, kudu rŭl an sasse yo. = Sangjŏm e katchi man, kudu rŭl an sasse yo.

Here are some past **-chi** forms:

chabŏtchi man	*caught but*
tadŏtchi man	*closed but*
usŏtchi man	*laughed but*
nohatchi man	*put but*
anjŭsŏtchi man	*someone honored sat but*
ssŏtchi man	*wrote but*

kasŏtchi man	*someone honored went but*
chuŏtchi man	*gave but*
pwatchi man	*saw but*
haetchi man	*did but*
kaji anhŏtchi man	*didn't go but*
oji anhŭsŏtchi man	*someone honored didn't come but*

Here are some examples in sentences :

Ŏje nŭn il haetchi man, onŭl ŭn swiŏ yo.	*Yesterday I worked but today I'm off (I rest).*
Sinmun ŭl pwatchi man, kŭ sajin ŭl an pwasse yo.	*I read the newspaper, but I didn't see that picture.*
Ch'aek ŭl ilgŏtchi man, yŏnghwa rŭl mot pwasse yo.	*I read the book, but I didn't get to see the picture.*
Yŏnghwa rŭl posiji an- h(ŭs)ŏtchi man, ch'aek ŭl ilgŭsŏsse yo ?	*You didn't see the movie, but you read the book ?*
Chip i chŏkchi man, ippŏ yo.	*The house is small but it's cute.*
Kae ga ippuji man, man- hi mŏgŏ yo.	*The dog is cute but he eats a lot.*
Na nŭn pyŏngjŏng iji man, ch'in-gu nŭn pyŏngjŏng i ani -e yo.	*I'm a soldier, but my friend isn't a soldier.*
Kim sŏnsaeng ŭn Han- guk (s)saram isiji man, Ma sŏnsaeng ŭn Chungguk (s)saram ise yo.	*Mr. Kim is a Korean, but Mr. Ma is Chinese.*
Na nŭn Ilbon sŏ watchi man, Ilbon (s)saram i ani -e yo.	*I came from Japan, but I'm not Japanese.*

Sikku ga manch'i man, ton i ŏpse yo.	*I have a big family, but I haven't any money.*
Nae ga ton ŭl chuŏtchi man, ta ssŭsŏsse yo.	*I gave you money but you spent it all.*

NOTE: **Ssŏ yo** means (1) *writes*, (2) *uses*, (3) *spends*, (4) *wears on head*. Below, **chagi** means *oneself*.

Moja rŭl ssŏtchi man, chagi moja ga ani -yŏsse yo.	*I put on a hat but it wasn't my own.*
Mannyŏnp'il i ŏpsŏtchi man, ch'in-gu ŭi yŏnp'il ŭl ssŏsse yo.	*I didn't have a pen, but I used a friend's pencil.*
Yŏnp'il lo ssŭsŏtchi man, kwaench'anhŏ yo.	*You wrote with a pencil, but it doesn't make any difference.*

Lesson 28

INFINITIVES—FAVORS

The infinitive is the form we get when we drop the particle **yo**: **pwa**, **hae**, **ka**, **mŏgŏ**, **anjŏ**, **nop'a**, **noha**, **ilgŏ**. But the infinitives of **isse yo**, **ŏpse yo** and **kat'e yo** are **issŏ**, **ŏpsŏ**, and **kat'ŏ**. (Some people say **issŏ yo** for **isse yo**, **ŏpsŏ yo** for **ŏpse yo**, and **kat'ŏ yo** for **kat'e yo**.) And the infinitives of honorific verbs which end in -(u)se yo have the ending -(ŭ)sŏ: **chapsuse yo** *someone honored eats* but **chapsusŏ**. There is also a past infinitive with the ending -ŏssŏ or **-assŏ** (with all the usual irregularities). The basic rule for making the infinitive from the base is this:

Add **-a** if the vowel of the preceding syllable is **o**, otherwise add **-ŏ**. But the infinitives of vowel bases are a bit more difficult, and the rules depend on which vowel the base ends in; it is probably easiest just to learn the infinitives without worrying how they are made.

The infinitive form is used in a great many ways. It should not be confused with the English form called infinitive—the two have little or nothing in common.

One way you will hear the infinitive form is all by itself at the end of a sentence in the FAMILIAR style. This style is just like the POLITE style you have learned, except that you drop the **yo** at the end (and usually change **-e** to **-ŏ**):

POLITE	FAMILIAR
Ŏdi sŏ wasse yo ?	Ŏdi sŏ wassŏ ?
Muŏs ŭl hase yo ?	Muŏs ŭl hasŏ ?
Kongjang e sŏ il hae yo.	Kongjang e sŏ il hae.
Ilgop si e mŏgŏ yo.	Ilgop si e mŏgŏ.
Kongbu haji anhŏ yo.	Kongbu haji anhŏ.

Another way to use the infinitive is in linking two verbs:

tora yo	*turns*
tora wa yo	*comes back, returns*
tora ka yo	*goes back, returns*
tŭrŏ yo	*enters*
tŭrŏ wa yo	*comes in*
tŭrŏ ka yo	*goes in*
na yo	*exits*

(69)

na wa yo	*comes out*
na ka yo	*goes out*
anjŏ yo	*sits*
anjŏ isse yo	*is seated*
nuwŏ yo	*lies down*
nuwŏ isse yo	*is lying, is prone*

With the verbs **chuŏ yo** *gives* and **tŭryŏ yo** *gives to someone honored*, this is the way to report a favor:

Abŏji ga p'yŏnji rŭl ssŏ chuŏsse yo.	*Father wrote the letter for me (he gave me the favor of writing the the letter).*
Ajumŏni ga ai hant'e yaegi rŭl hae chuŏsse yo.	*The aunt told the children a story.*
Adŭl i abŏji ŭi kudu rŭl takkŏ tŭryŏsse yo.	*The boy shined his father's shoes (for him).*

The person FOR whom the favor is done is the INDIRECT OBJECT and takes the particle **hant'e** (or its equivalents **eke** or **pogo**, or its honorific equivalent **kke**).

To ask someone for a favor you can use the infinitive **chuse yo** (*someone honored,* that is YOU) *please give* or the Formal style command **chusipsio** *please give*:

Ton ŭl chuse yo. Ton ŭl chusipsio.	*Please give me some money.*
Ton ŭl nae chusipsio.	*Please (do me the favor of) pay(ing) the money.*
Maeil uri chip e wa chusipsio.	*Please come to our house tomorrow.*
Chom tŏ chapsuŏ chusipsio.	*Please eat a little more.*

Yaegi rŭl hae chuse yo.	*Tell us a story.*
Mannyŏnp'il lo ssŭ chuse yo.	*Please write with pen and ink.*
I kŏs ŭl padŏ chusipsio.	*Please take (accept) this.*
Yŏgi noha chuse yo.	*Put it here, please.*

To make a negative request you use the **-chi** (or **-ŭsiji**) form followed by the auxiliary verb **mase yo** *avoid* or its Formal style command form **masipsio**:

Yŏngŏ ro haji mase yo. Yŏngŏ ro haji masipsio.	*Don't speak English.*
Kŏgi anjŭsiji masipsio.	*Don't sit there.*
Yŏnp'il lo ssŭji mase yo.	*Don't write with a pencil.*
I kŏs ŭl saji mase yo.	*Don't buy this.*

Lesson 29

" MAY " AND " MUST "

The infinitive + **to** means *even though*. Sometimes this is similar to the meaning of **-chi man** *but*.

| Ton i ŏpsŏ to, kippŏ yo. | *Even though I have no money I am happy.* |
| Ton i ŏpchi man, kippŏ yo. | *I have no money, but I am happy.* |

Usually you use a present infinitive in front of **to** even if the meaning is past, because the sentence makes this clear.

Ch'aek i ŏpsŏ to, hak-kyo e kasse yo.	*I went to school even though I didn't have my book.*
Kŭ yŏnghwa ga cho-ch'i anhŏ to, chip e tora kaji anhŏsse yo.	*Even though the movie was no good, I didn't go home.*
Na nŭn kŭ yŏja ga choha to, kŭ yŏja nŭn na rŭl choha haji anhŏsse yo.	*Even though I liked that girl, she didn't like me.*
Kyŏlhon hae to, kip-pŭji anhŏsse yo.	*Even though we got married, we weren't happy.*

This construction is used in asking or giving PERMISSION. To say *may I, can I, will you let me, is it OK to* the Korean says something like *even if I do it, is it all right?* or *even though I do it, does it make any difference?* The word for all right is **choha yo** *is good* or **kwaench'anhŏ yo** *makes no difference.*

Iltchigi wa to choha yo?	*Is it all right if I come early?*
Taek kkaji kach'i ka to kwaench'anhŏ yo?	*May I walk home (together) with you?*
Nae ga ton ŭl nae to choha yo?	*Will you let me pay?*
Onul (p)pam nŭtke tora wa to kwaench' anhŏ yo.	*You can (I can) come back late tonight.*
I pang an e kesŏ to choha yo.	*You may stay in this room.*
Yŏgi anjŏ to kwaench'-anhŏ yo.	*You can sit here.*

To express OBLIGATION, you use the infinitive (or

the honorific infinitive)+**ya hae yo** which means something like *has to, must, has got to*. The particle **ya** has a meaning something like *only if you do* and the **hae yo** means (*then*) *it will do*. In other words *only if you...will it do=you have to...*

Onŭl (p)pam iltchigi tora osŏ ya hae yo.	*You have to come back early tonight.*
Chal kongbu hae ya hae yo.	*I have to study hard (or well).*
Hakkyo e ka ya hae yo?	*Do I have to go to school?*
Ton ŭl nae ya hae yo?	*Do I have to pay the money?*
I ch'aek ŭl pwa ya hae yo.	*I've got to read this book.*
I pang an e kesŏ ya hae yo.	*You have to stay in this room.*
Yŏgi anjŏ ya hae yo?	*Do I have to sit here?*
I kŏs ŭl mŏgŏ ya hae yo?	*Do I have to eat this?*
Kŭ kongjang e sŏ il ŭl manhi hae ya haesse yo.	*We had to do a lot of work at that factory.*
Ŏje ŏdi ŏdi kasŏ ya haesse yo?	*Yesterday where all (where and where) did you have to go?*
Sae mannyŏnp'il ŭl sa ya hae yo.	*I have to buy a new pen.*
Chigŭm ŭn nae ga muŏs ŭl hae ya hae yo?	*What do I have to do now?*

To deny obligation *you don't have to, you need not,* you say something like *it's all right even if you don't* : **-chi anhŏ to choha yo** or **-chi anhŏ to kwaench' anhŏ yo.**

Iltchigi tora osiji anhŏ to kwaench'anhŏ yo.	*You don't have to come back early.*

(73)

Hakkyo e an ka to choha yo.	*You don't have to go to school.*
I ch'aek ŭl poji anhŏ to kwaench'anhŏ yo.	*I don't have to read this book.*
Kŏgi antchi anhŭsŏ to choha yo.	*You don't have to sit there. (It's OK if you don't sit there.)*
Sae mannyŏnp'il ŭl saji anhŏ to kwaench'anhŏ yo.	*You don't have to buy a new pen.*
Kŭ p'yŏnji nŭn chigŭm ssŭji anhŏ to choch'i man, i p'yŏnji nŭn kkok ssŏ ya hae yo.	*That letter doesn't have to be written now, but this letter I have to write for sure (kkok).*

Lesson 30

AUXILIARY VERBS

You have learned that the verbs **chuŏ yo** *gives* and **tŭryŏ yo** *gives to someone honored* have special meanings following an infinitive: *does the favor of doing, does FOR someone.*

Verbs which have special meanings of this sort when used with other verbs are called AUXILIARY VERBS. Most auxiliary verbs are used in combination with the infinitive form, but some are used with other forms.

The verb **pwa yo** ordinarily means *looks, sees, reads* but as an auxiliary it means *tries doing*—NOT *tries* TO *do* but *tries do*ING, that is, *samples the act to see what it's like*:

Han-guk mal lo p'yŏnji rŭl ssŏ pwasse yo.	*I tried writing a letter in Korean.*
Han-guk sinmun ŭl pwa pwasse yo.	*I tried reading a Korean newspaper.*
Na nŭn ch'ŏnch'ŏnhi mal hae pwatchi man, kŭ saram i ihae haji mot haesse yo.	*I tried talking slowly, but he couldn't understand me.*
Han-guk ŭmsik chom chapsŭŏ pwa chusipsio.	*Try eating a little Korean food.*

This exploratory construction -ŏ **pwa yo** is often used with *going* and *coming*:

Ilbon e ka posŏsse yo ?	*Have you been to Japan? (Did you try going to Japan? Did you go to Japan to see how things are there?)*
Nae ch'in-gu ga naeil i kongwŏn e wa pwa yo.	*My friend is coming to (see) this park tomorrow.*

The verb **pŏryŏ yo** means *throws away, discards*:

Wae i kabang ŭl pŏrisŏsse yo ?	*Why did you throw away this briefcase?*

As an auxiliary it means *does something completely, for good; puts an end to something*. The initial **p** doubles when the verb is linked to the preceding infinitive:

Yŏlssoe rŭl ilhŏ ppŏryŏsse yo.	*I lost the key.*

(75)

Uri chip e kae ga issŏt- chi man,tu tal chŏn e chugŏ ppŏryŏsse yo.

We had a dog at our house, but it died 2 months ago.

Ton ŭl ta ssŏ ppŏrisŏsse yo?

Did you spend all the money?

Ch'am-mal Miguk e tora ka ppŏrise yo?

Are you really going back to America (for good)?

The verb tuŏ yo means: *puts away (for a long time), gets out of the way, stores:*

Pom i wasse yo. Kyŏul os ŭl ŏdi tuŏ yo?

Spring has come; where do we put the winter clothes?

Kaŭl i wasse yo. Wae yŏrŭm (k)kŏs ŭl ajik tuji anhŏsse yo?

Fall has come. Why haven't you stored the summer things yet?

Ŭmsing-mul ŭl i kwang an e tuŏ yo.

We keep foodstuff in this store-room.

Kŭ chapchi nŭn tosŏ-sil e tuŏsse yo.

They put those magazines in the library (room).

As an auxiliary, tuŏ yo means *gets something done that has to be done, does something up:*

Ŏmŏni ga os ŭl pparŏ tuŏsse yo.

Mother washed the clothes, got the laundry done.

Kŭ taŭm e, chip an ŭl soje hae tuŏsse yo.

Then, (next) she cleaned (inside) the house.

Kŭ hu e harabŏji hant'e p'yŏnji rŭl ssŏ tuŏsse yo.

After that she got a letter written to grandfather.

The verb noha yo means *puts aside (for later use), lays something somewhere (with the expectation of using it again later).* As an auxiliary it means something like *does for later; gets something done (so that it will be ready for later use):*

(76)

Maeil (k)kongbu rŭl ŏje (p)pam hae nohasse yo.	*I did tomorrow's lesson (studying) last night.*
Kŭmyoil chŏn e i ch'aek ŭl ilgŏ nohŭse yo.	*Please read this book by Friday.*
Met si e ŭmsik ŭl maendŭrŏ nohŭse yo?	*What time are you getting the meal ready?*
Sae kongch'aek ŭl sa nohasse yo.	*I bought a new notebook (to use).*
P'yo rŭl chigŭm sa noha to choha yo?	*Can we buy the tickets now (in advance)?*

Lesson 31

THE GERUND OR -ko FORM

A very common verb form is the gerund or -ko (-go) form. This has a number of uses and we can give it the tag translations of *doing* or *does and, is and.* The form is made by adding -ko (or -go) to the verb base in much the same way that -chi (or -ji) is added. Note that tk usually sounds like kk.

MEANING	BASE	-CHI FORM	-KO FORM
catches	chab-	chapchi	chapko
is high	nop'-	nopchi	nopko
is nonexistent	ŏps-	ŏpchi	ŏpko
closes	tad-	tatchi	tatko (-kk-)
is like	kat'-	katchi	katko (-kk-)
laughs	us-	utchi	utko (-kk-)
exists	iss-	itchi	itko (-kk-)

(77)

finds	ch'aj-	ch'atchi	ch'atko (-kk-)
washes	ssich'-	ssitchi	ssitko (-kk-)
reads	ilg-	ikchi	ilkko or ikko
loses	ilh-	ilch'i	ilk'o
licks	halt'-	haltchi	halkko
steps on	palb-	paltchi	palkko
chants	ŭlp'-	ŭltchi	ŭlkko
puts	noh-	noch'i	nok'o
eats	mŏg-	mŏkchi	mŏkko
cuts	kkakk-	kkakchi	kkakko
shampoos	kam-	kamtchi	kamkko
is young	chŏlm-	chŏmtchi	chŏmkko
wears on feet	sin-	sintchi	sinkko
sits	anj-	antchi	ankko
breaks	kkŭnh-	kkŭnch'i	kkŭnk'o
equals, is	(i)-	iji, -ji	igo, -go
rests	swi-	swiji	swigo
(honorific)	-(ŭ)si-	-(ŭ)siji	-(ŭ)sigo
pays	nae-	naeji	naego
writes	ssŭ-	ssŭji	ssŭgo
goes	ka-	kaji	kago
gives	chu-	chuji	chugo
sees	po-	poji	pogo
does	ha-	haji	hago

One use of the gerund to mean *doing* is with the auxiliary **isse yo** *is* or **kese yo** *someone honored is*:

Abŏji ga mun ŭl tatko isse yo.	*Father is shutting the door.*
Aegi ga utko issŏsse yo.	*The baby was laughing.*
Musŭn ch'aek ŭl ilkko kese yo?	*What book are you reading?*
Ai tŭl i chigŭm pap ŭl mŏkko itchi man, kŭ	*The children are eating (their food) now, but afterward*

(78)

hu e kongwŏn e san-	it's all right for them to go
ppo ka to kwaench'an-	to the park for a walk.
hŏ yo.	
Kŭ nal swigo issŏsse yo.	I was off (resting) that day.
Kongbu rŭl hago kese	Are you doing your lesson?
yo?	
Yŏpsŏ rŭl ssŭgo isse yo.	I'm writing a postcard.

Notice that some verbs have slightly different meanings in the *is doing* form:

ibŏ yo	puts on (clothes), wears
ipko isse yo	is wearing
ssŏ yo	puts on (hat), wears (hat)
ssŭgo isse yo	is wearing (hat)
sinŏ yo	puts on (shoes, socks), wears (shoes, socks)
sinkko isse yo	is wearing (shoes, socks)
Kŭ chapchi rŭl ch'atko	I was LOOKING FOR that mag-
issŏtchi man, ch'atchi	azine, but I couldn't FIND
mot haesse yo.	it.

The second use of the gerund is in the meaning *does and (then)* or *is and (also)*:

Os ŭl ipko, kudu rŭl	I put on clothes, shoes, and
sinkko, moja rŭl ssŏ	hat.
yo.	
I kŏs ŭn nae moja -go,	This is my hat and that is
kŭ kos ŭn adŭl ŭi	my son's.
moja -e yo.	

You could say these ideas in short, abrupt sentences using the connective word **kŭrigo** *does and, is and*:

Os ŭl ibŏ yo: Kŭrigo, kudu rŭl sinŏ yo: Kŭrigo
moja rŭl ssŏ yo. I kŏs ŭn nae moja -e yo: Kŭrigo,
kŭ kŏs ŭn adŭl ŭi moja -e yo.

(79)

To say *did and then; was and (also)* you can use
the ordinary gerund, letting the final past form carry
the meaning throughout:

Os ŭl ipko, kudu rŭl sinkko, moja rŭl ssŏsse yo.	*I put on my clothes, my shoes, and my hat.*
I kŏs ŭn nae moja -go, kŭ kŏs ŭn atŭl ŭi moja -yŏsse yo.	*This was my hat, and that was my son's.*

Or, you can use a special past gerund (-ŏtko, -atko,
with the usual irregularities of the infinitive -ŏ, -a
and the past -ŏss-, -ass-):

Os ŭl ibŏtko, kudu rŭl sinŏtko, moja rŭl ssŏsse yo.
I kŏs ŭn nae moja -yŏtko, kŭ kŏs ŭn adŭl ŭi moja
-yŏsse yo.

Lesson 32

WANTS AND LIKES

To say *I want to ......* or *I would like to ......* use
the gerund form of the verb followed by the auxiliary
sip'ŏ yo *is desired*:

Nae ga kŭ yŏnghwa rŭl pogo sip'ŏ yo.	*I want to see that movie.*
Kŭ yŏja rŭl mannago sip'ŏ yo.	*I want to meet that girl.*

Taek ŭl pangmun hago sip'ŏ yo.	*I want to visit your house.*
Na nŭn yŏgi sŏ chago sip'ŏ yo.	*I want to sleep here.*
Munsan e ka pogo sip'ŏ yo.	*I want to go to (see) Munsan.*
Tambae rŭl sago sip'ŏ yo.	*I want to buy some cigarettes.*
Tambae rŭl p'igo sip'ŏ yo.	*I want to smoke (cigarettes).*
Ton ŭl patko sip'ŏ yo.	*I want to get some money.*
Tta nim hant'e sŏnmul ŭl tŭrigo sip'ŏ yo.	*I want to give your daughter a gift.*
Chikkŭm mŏkko sip'ŏ yo!	*I want to eat right now!*
Kidarigo sipchi anhŏ yo.	*I don't want to wait.*
Yaegi rŭl hae tŭrigo sip'ŏ yo.	*I want to tell you a story.*
Onŭl p'yo rŭl sa nok'o sip'ŏ yo.	*I want to buy the tickets today (in advance).*
Pohi hago kach'i sanppo hago sip'ŏ yo.	*I want to take a walk with Pohi.*
Abŏ nim hago kach'i yaegi rŭl hago sip'ŏ yo.	*I want to have a talk with your father.*
Kim sŏnsaeng hant'e mal hago sip'ŏ yo.	*I want to speak to Mr. Kim.*
Na nŭn chip e tora ka-go sip'ŏ yo.	*I want to go home.*
Na nŭn Han-guk e itko sip'ŏ yo.	*I want to stay in Korea.*
Ilbon e tora kago sip-chi anhŏ yo.	*I don't want to go back to Japan.*

But to say someone other than yourself *wants to*

you usually use **sip'ŏ hae yo** instead of **sip'ŏ yo**. You can use **sip'ŏ hae yo** to mean *I want to* but it's rather strong like *I'm longing to* :

Pohi ga kŭ yŏnghwa rŭl posigo sip'ŏ hae yo? (or ...... pogo sip'ŏ hase yo? or ... ... posigo sip'ŏ hase yo?)	*Do you, Pohi, want to see that movie?*
Nu ga yŏgi sŏ chago sip'ŏ hae yo?	*Who wants to sleep here?*
Chungguk ŭmsik ŭl chapsusigo sip'ŏ hase yo?	*Do you want to eat Chinese food?*
Abŏ nim i na hago kach'i yaegi rŭl hago sip'ŏ hase yo?	*Does your father want to have a talk with me?*
Kŭ ae rŭl mannago sip'o hase yo?	*Do you want to meet her?*

(**Kŭ ae** *that child* is used as a somewhat familiar form of **kŭ saram** *that person*.)

Kim sŏnsaeng i onŭl ppam osigo sip'o hasiji anhŏ yo.	*Mr Kim doesn't want to come tonight.*
Aegi ga sŏnsaeng hago nolgo sip'ŏ hae yo.	*The baby wants to play with you.*
Uri chip e sŏ nolgo sip'ŏ hasiji anhŏ yo?	*Don't you want to have a visit at our house?*

(**Nora yo** *plays, visits, has good time, amuses self.*)

Chom tŏ kidarisigo sip'ŏ hase yo?	*Do you want to wait a bit more?*
Poktongi ga pap ŭl mŏkko sip'ŏ haji anhŏ yo.	*Poktongi doesn't want to eat his food.*

| Ai tŭl i chago sip'ŏ haji anhŏ yo. | *The children don't want to go to bed.* |

To say *someone likes something* you use the expression choha hae yo :

Sŏnsaeng i kŭ yŏnghwa rŭl choha hasŏsse yo ?	*Did you like that movie ?*
Kkoch' ŭl choha hase yo ?	*Do you like flowers ?*
Uri ttal ŭl choha hase yo ?	*Do you like my (our) daughter ?*
Ttal i sanppo rŭl choha hae yo.	*She (the daughter) likes (to take) walks.*
Na rŭl choha hase yo ?	*Do you like me ?*
Han-guk ŭi kŏs ŭl choha hase yo ?	*Do you like Korean things ?*
Aegi tŭl i uyu rŭl choha hae yo.	*Babies like milk.*
Kwaengi to uyu rŭl choha haji anhŏ yo ?	*Don't cats like milk, too ?*

To say *I like something* you can use the above expression, or you can use a somewhat weaker (and more sophisticated) expression which means something like *as for me, the thing is liked* :

Nae ga kŭ yŏnghwa ga choha yo.	*I like that movie.*
Na nŭn tta nim i choha yo.	*I like your daughter.*
Na nŭn Han-guk yŏja tŭl i choha yo.	*I like Korean women.*
Na nŭn Pohi ga choha yo.	*I like you, Pohi.*
Na nŭn yŏgi ga choha yo.	*I like this place.*

| **I ŭmsik i choha yo.** | *I like this food.* |
| **Na nŭn Ilbon i chohasse yo.** | *I liked Japan.* |

The verb **choha yo** has three meanings : (1) *is good*, (2) *is liked*, (3) *am happy*.

The expression **choha hae yo** has two meanings : (1) *likes*, (2) *is happy*.

Notice that the THING you like takes the particle **i/ga** with the expression **choha yo** ; but the particle **ŭl/rŭl** is more common with **choha hae yo**.

To say *I like* TO DO *something* you have to use a special form of the verb in front of **choha yo** or **choha hae yo**. This is the **-ki** (or **-gi**) form. The ending is added to the bases just like the gerund **-ko** (or **-go**) form :

Nae ga yŏnghwa rŭl pogi choha yo.	*I like to see movies.*
Ttal i Miguk saram ŭl mannagi choha hae yo.	*My daughter likes meeting Americans.*
Ai tŭl i sŏnmul ŭl patki choha hae yo.	*The children like to get presents.*
Harabŏji ga yŏhaeng ŭl hagi choha haesse yo.	*My grandfather used to like making trips.*
Anhae ga yŏhaeng hagi choha haji anhŏ yo.	*My wife doesn't like to travel.*
Chip e itki choha hae yo.	*She likes to stay at home.*
Nae ga Han-guk chip e sŏ nolgi choha yo.	*I like to visit in Korean homes.*
Chungguk ŭmsikchŏm e sŏ chinji rŭl chapsusigi choha hase yo ?	*Do you like to eat in Chinese restaurants ?*

(84)

Notice that *I* WOULD LIKE *to* is not the same as *I* LIKE *to*.

I WOULD *like to* means *I* WANT *to*, **-ko sip'ŏ yo.**

I LIKE *to* means *it is pleasant for me to*, **-ki choha yo.**

You may be puzzled why you don't hear the **h** in **choha yo** and **noha yo**. **H** between voiced sounds frequently disappears, and in verb forms like these it usually isn't pronounced at all. You may even hear a **w**-like sound between the **o** and the **a** and want to write the words **chowa yo** and **nowa yo**.

Lesson 33

INFINITIVE + so — " AND SO "

When the particle **sŏ** follows the infinitive, the meaning is something like *does and so, is and so* or just *does and, is and*:

Ton i ŏpsŏ sŏ, mot ka yo.	*I haven't any money so I can't go.*

This could be broken up into more abrupt sentences with the connective expression **Kŭrae sŏ**:

Ton i ŏpse yo. Kŭrae sŏ, mot ka yo.

For the past *did and so, was and so* you usually just use the plain infinitive + **sŏ**, since the final verb

(85)

shows that the meaning is past. There is a past
infinitive (-ŏssŏ, -assŏ etc.) which can be used to make
the pastness explicit :

Pae ga kop'a sŏ, ŭm- *I was hungry so I went into*
sikchŏm e tŭrŏ kasse *the restaurant.*
yo.

Pae ga kop'assŏ sŏ, kŭ *He was hungry so he stole the*
ŭmsik ŭl humch'ŏsse *food.*
yo.

    (**Pae** *stomach.* **Pae ga kop'a yo** *is hungry.*
    Humch'ŏ yo *steals.* The base of **kop'a**
    yo is **kop'ŭ-** ; of **humch'ŏ yo, humch'i-**.)

Mok i mallŏ sŏ, mul ŭl *I was thirsty so I drank some*
masŏsse yo. *water.*

    (**Mok** *throat,* **Mallŏ yo** *gets dry, is dry.*
    Drinks is either **mŏgŏ yo** or **masŏ yo** ; the
    base of **masŏ yo** is **masi-**.)

Here are some more examples :

Ttal hago kyŏlhon hago *I wanted to marry the daugh-*
sip'ŏssŏ sŏ, kŭ abŏji *ter, so I had to talk with*
hago yaegi rŭl hae *her father.*
ya haesse yo.

Han-guk yŏkssa rŭl *I want to study Korea's history,*
kongbu hago sip'ŏ sŏ, *so I am going to Seoul*
Sŏul Taehak e tanigo *University.*
isse yo.

    (**Tanyŏ yŏ** *goes regularly, goes back*
    and forth, keeps going. Base **tani-**.)

Chigŭm chip e tora ka *I have to go home now, so I*
ya hae sŏ, chadongch'a *am looking for a taxi (auto-*
rŭl ch'atko isse yo. *mobile).*

Nae ga kkoch' i choha *I like flowers, so I take a*
sŏ, nal mada kongwŏn *walk in the park every day.*
e sŏ sanppo rŭl hae
yo.

Kkot pat' i mŏrŏ sŏ, kŏrŏ kaji mot hae yo.	The flower gardens are far away so I can't walk.
Nae hakkyo ga chip e sŏ kakkawŏ sŏ kŏrŏ ka to choha yo.	My school is near (from) the house, so I can walk.

(Kŏrŏ ka yo *walks, goes on foot.*
Kŏrŏ wa yo *walks, comes on foot.*)

Kongwŏn ŭn kakkap-chi anhŏ sŏ, chŏnch'a ro ka ya hae yo.	The park isn't near, so I have to go by streetcar.
Uri chip i jŏnggŏjang e sŏ mŏlji anhŏ sŏ, kŏgi sŏ kŏrŏ wa to choha yo.	Our house isn't far from the station, so you can come from there on foot.
Chadongch'a rŭl t'aji anhŏ to kwaench'-anhŏ yo.	You don't have to take a taxi.
Kich'a rŭl t'ago ogo sip'ŏtchi man, ŏpsŏsse yo.	I wanted to come (riding) on a train, but there wasn't any.
Chadongch'a rŭl t'ago tora kase yo.	Go home in a cab.

T'a yo *takes (a vehicle).* T'ago ka yo *goes in (a vehicle).* T'ago wa yo *comes in (a vehicle).* Compare: Pihaengi ro wasse yo. *I came by plane.* Pihaengi rŭl t'ago wasse yo. *I came on a plane.*

The infinitive+sŏ means *does and* in expressions like *goes and does* or *comes and does*:

Sangjŏm e ka sŏ, silgwa rŭl sasse yo.	He went to the store and bought some fruit.
Onŭl ach'im nae ga to-sŏgwan e ka sŏ, ch'aek ŭl pillyŏ yo.	This morning I'm going to the library (building) and borrow a book.

Kim sowi ga uri chip e wa sŏ, chadongch'a rŭl pilligo kyŏngch'al e kasse yo.	*Lt. Kim came to my place and borrowed the car and went to the police.*

The expression -ŏ sŏ choha yo means *I'm glad that*; -ŏ sŏ choha hae yo means someone else *is glad that*:

Tta nim to osŏ sŏ (nae ga) choha yo.	*I'm glad your daughter came, too.*
Kŭ yŏnghwa rŭl pwa sŏ, ai tŭl i choha haesse yo.	*The children were glad they saw that movie.*
I ch'aek ŭl ilgŏ sŏ choha yo.	*I'm glad I read this book.*
Han-guk mal ŭl kongbu hasŏ sŏ choha hase yo?	*Are you glad you studied Korean?*
Sikku ga manch'i anhŏ sŏ choha yo.	*I'm glad there aren't many in my family.*
Ton i chŏkchi anhŏ sŏ choha yo.	*I'm glad we have quite a bit of money (...... that the money is not little).*
Uri hakkyo tosŏsil i ch'aek i chŏkchi anhŏ sŏ, sŏnsaeng nim tŭl i choha hase yo.	*The teachers are happy that our school library room has quite a few books (...... that the books are not few).*

Lesson 34

SOME PECULIAR VERB TYPES

Verb bases with the basic form ending in **w** change
this **w** to **p** or **u** in certain forms:

tow-	*help*
towa yo	*helps*
topchi anhŏ yo	*doesn't help*
topko isse yo	*is helping*
touse yo	*(someone honored) helps*
topko kese yo or **tousigo kese yo**	*(someone honored) is helping*

Here are some of these verbs:

nuwŏ yo	*lies down*
swiwŏ yo	*is easy*
ŏryŏwŏ yo	*is difficult*
ch'uwŏ yo	*is cold*
kakkawŏ yo	*is near*
arŭmdawŏ yo	*is beautiful*
kowa yo	*is pretty*
tŏwŏ yo	*is warm*
maewŏ yo	*is hot-tasting, spicy*
pan-gawŏ yo	*is happy*
komawŏ yo	*is grateful*

Most of these verbs correspond to English adjectives;
they mean IS *something* rather than DOES *something*.

Verb bases ending in **l** or **r** are of two types : regular consonant **r**-bases, and **l**-extending vowel bases. In the first type, the **r** is replaced by **t** in certain forms :

kŏr-	*walk*
kŏrŏ yo	*walks*
kŏtchi anhŏ yo	*doesn't walk*
kŏtko isse yo	*is walking*
kŏrŭse yo	*(someone honored) walks*
kŏtko kese yo or kŏrŭsigo kese yo	*(someone honored) is walking*

In the second type, the **l** (or **r**) is an extension which the base acquires before you attach certain endings :

kŏ-l-	*hang*
kŏrŏ yo	*hangs*
kŏlji anhŏ yo	*doesn't hang*
kŏlgo isse yo	*is hanging*
kŏse yo	*(someone honored) hangs*
kŏlgo kese yo or kŏsigo kese yo	*(someone honored) is hanging*

You will notice that some of the forms of the consonant **r**-bases are the same as those of the **l**-extending vowel bases :

	CONSONANT BASE	VOWEL BASE	CONSONANT BASE	VOWEL BASE
BASE	kŏr- walk	kŏ-l- hang	tŭr- listen	tŭ-l- enter
PRESENT	kŏrŏ yo	kŏrŏ yo	tŭrŏ yo	tŭrŏ yo
PAST	kŏrŏsse yo	kŏrŏsse yo	tŭrosse yo	tŭrŏsse yo
HON.	kŏrŭse yo	kŏse yo	tŭrŭse yo	tŭse yo
HON. PAST	kŏrŭsŏsse yo	kŏsŏsse yo	tŭrŭsŏsse yo	tŭsŏsse yo
-CHI	kŏtchi	kŏlji	tŭtchi	tŭlji
GERUND	kŏtko	kŏlgo	tŭtko	tŭlgo

Here are some consonant bases ending in **r**:

mur :	*inquire,* murŭ yo, mutchi anhŏ yo, mutko
tar :	*run,* tarŭ yo, tatchi anhŏ yo, tatko
sir :	*be loaded with,* sirŭ yo, sitchi anhŏ yo, sitko
kkaedar :	*realize,* kkaedarŭ yo, kkaedatchi anhŏ yo, kkaedatko

Here are some l-extending vowel bases:

ki-l :	*be long,* kirŭ yo, kilji anhŏ yo, kilgo
a-l :	*know, find out,* arŭ yo, algo
sa-l :	*live,* sarŭ yo, salji anhŏ yo, salgo
u-l :	*cry,* urŭ yo, ulji anhŏ yo, ulgo
no-l :	*play, visit, enjoy,* nora yo, nolji anhŏ yo, nolgo
yŏ-l :	*open,* yŏrŭ yo, yŏlji anhŏ yo, yŏlgo
pu-l :	*blow,* purŭ yo, pulji anhŏ yo, pulgo
ppa-l :	*launder,* pparŭ yo, ppalji anhŏ yo, ppalgo

NOTE: The negative of **arŭ yo** is a special verb **molla yo** *does not know.* (Base **moru-**.) Examples of some of these verbs follow:

Nae ga kil ŭl molla sŏ, chunsa hant'e murŭ pwasse yo.	*I didn't know the road, so I asked (tried inquiring of) a policeman.*
Namu mit' e sŏ taramjwi ga tatko isse yo.	*Squirrels are running under the trees.*
Poktongi ga abŏji sori rŭl tŭtko, tarŭ wasse yo.	*Poktongi heard his father's voice and came running.*
Ulji mase yo.	*Don't cry.*
Kŭ kŏs ŭl kkaedatchi mot haesse yo.	*I hadn't realized that.*
Pae ga ch'ong hago ch'ong-al ŭl sirŭ yo.	*The boat is carrying rifles and bullets.*
Nugu hant'e sŏ kŭ kŏs ŭl arŏsse yo ?	*Who did you find that out from?*

Kil i kirŏ to, kŏrŏ ka ya hae yo.	*Even though the road is long, we'll have to walk.*
Yŏgi nupji mase yo.	*Don't lie down here.*
Na rŭl towa chuse yo.	*Help me.*
Nal i nŏmu tŏwŏ sŏ, chago sip'ŏ yo.	*The weather (day) is too warm, so I want to sleep; The weather is so warm I want to sleep.*
Nŏmu ch'uwŏ sŏ, oet'u rŭl ibŏ ya hae yo.	*The weather is so cold you have to wear an overcoat.*
Han-guk mal i swipchi anhŏ yo.	*Korean isn't easy.*
Yŏng-ŏ to ŏryŏwŏ yo.	*English is difficult, too.*
I ŭmsik i nŏmu maewŏ sŏ, mot mŏgŏ yo.	*This food is so hot-tasting, I can't eat it.*
Sŏnsaeng ŭl manna sŏ, ch'am pan-gawŏ yo.	*I am very happy to meet you.*

Lesson 35

MODIFIERS: -ŭn / -n

In English we have expressions like *the man* THAT *came yesterday* or *the man* WHO *came yesterday*, *the man* THAT *I saw yesterday* or *the man* WHO(M) *I saw yesterday*. These are called relative clauses and usually contain a relative pronoun—*who, which, that, where* —though this is sometimes omitted: *the man I saw yesterday*.

In the equivalent Korean expression, there is no

relative pronoun, and the relative clause goes in front of the noun it modifies; you say something like *the came-yesterday man*, *the I-saw-yesterday man*. The verb in these modifying constructions appears in a special form we shall call the MODIFIER form.

The ordinary modifier form has the ending **-ŭn** after a consonant base, **-n** after a vowel base:

anjŭn saram	*the man who sat down*
on saram	*the man who came*

The meaning of the modifier form depends on whether the Korean verb corresponds to an English verb or an English adjective; in other words, whether the verb means DOES *something* or IS *something*. The meaning of the modifier form with PROCESS verbs (*does something*) is ...... *that has done* or ...... *that someone has done*: **pon saram** *the man that saw* or *the man that someone saw*.

To make it clear which of these two meanings is involved you have to give the verb either a subject or an object:

Kim sŏnsaeng ŭl pon saram	*The man that saw Mr. Kim*
Kim sŏnsaeng i pon saram	*The man that Mr. Kim saw*

Then you can take the whole expression and make it the subject, object, or whatnot of a larger sentence, by putting an appropriate particle after the noun:

Kim sŏnsaeng i pon saram i nae ch'in-gu -e yo.	*The man Mr. Kim saw is my friend.*

(93)

Kim sŏnsaeng ŭl pon saram i nae ch'in-gu -e yo.	*The man who saw Mr. Kim is my friend.*
Kim sŏnsaeng i pon saram ŭl na to pwasse yo.	*I too saw the man Mr. Kim saw.*
Kim sŏnsaeng ŭl pon saram i na to pwasse yo.	*The man who saw Mr. Kim saw me too.*
Kim sŏnsaeng i pon saram hant'e sŏ ton ŭl padŏsse yo.	*Mr. Kim got money from the man he saw.*
Kim sŏnsaeng ŭl pon saram hant'e sŏ (Kim sŏnsaeng i) ton ŭl padŏsse yo.	*Mr. Kim got money from the man who saw him.*

Compare the following sets of sentences :

Kŭ saram i tosŏgwan e sŏ ch'aek ŭl pillyŏsse yo.	*That person borrowed a book from the library.*
Tosŏgwan e sŏ ch'aek ŭl pillin (kŭ) saram i nugu -yŏsse yo ?	*Who was the person who borrowed a book from the library ?*
Kŭ saram i tosŏgwan e sŏ pillin ch'aek i mu-sŭn ch'aek iŏsse yo ?	*What was the book that person borrowed from the library ?*
Pyŏngjŏng i mun ŭl tadŏsse yo.	*A soldier closed the door.*
Mun ŭl tadŭn pyŏng-jŏng i Miguk (s)saram iŏsse yo ?	*Was the soldier who closed the door an American ?*
Pyŏngjŏng i tadŭn mun ŭn ap mun ie yo ?	*Is it the front door that the soldier closed ?*

The meaning of the modifier form with DESCRIPTION

verbs (*is something*) is simply ...... *that is*:

khŭn chip	*a house that is big = a big house*
mŏn tosi	*a city that is far away = a far-away city*
kakkaun hakkyo	*a school that is nearby = a nearby school*
chŏlmŭn saram	*a person who is young = a young person*
kunin in saram tŭl	*people who are servicemen*
moksa -sin pun	*a(n honored) man who is a preacher*
kin kil	*a road that is long = a long road*
tchalbŭn kil	*a road that is short = a short road*
pulgŭn moja	*a hat that is red = a red hat*
hin ot	*clothes that are white = white clothes*
kŏmŭn kudu	*black shoes*
p'urŭn hanul	*blue sky*
chohŭn nal	*nice day, nice weather*
nappŭn ilgi	*bad weather*
nop'ŭn san	*high mountains*
najŭn ŏndŏk	*low hill*
koun saekssi	*a pretty girl*
ch'uun pam	*a cold night*
chŏgŭn ai	*a small child*

These expressions can then be made the subject, object, or whatnot of larger sentences:

Koun saekssi rŭl man-nasse yo.	*I met a pretty girl.*
Koun saekssi ga na wa kach'i sanppo haesse yo.	*The pretty girl took a walk with me.*

| Koun saekssi ŭi chip ŭl pangmun haesse yo. | *I visited the pretty girl's house.* |
| Koun saekssi hant'e sŏ nal mada p'yŏnji rŭl padŏ yo. | *I get a letter from the pretty girl every day.* |

The possibilities, you can see, are endless.

In Lesson 36 you will find a list of modifiers for typical verb shapes.

Lesson 36

PROCESSIVE MODIFIERS: -nŭn

Pwa yo means either *looks at*, *sees* or *reads*. (*Sees a person* is often **manna yo** *meets.*) But to say *the man who is reading* or *the book that the man is reading* you can't used **pon** because **pon saram** means *the man who has read* and **pon ch'aek** means *the book someone has read.*

Instead, there is a special form, the PROCESSIVE modifier, used only with process verbs (DOES *something*). This form is made by adding the ending -nŭn to the verb base. (Various sound changes take place automatically when you attach the ending to a consonant base.) So we have sentences like:

| Ch'aek ŭl ponŭn saram i nugu -e yo? | *Who is the man (who is) reading the book?* |

Ch'aek ŭl ponŭn saram ŭl mannasse yo?	*Have you met the man who is reading the book? Did you see a man reading a book?*
Kŭ saram i ponŭn ch'aek i musŭn ch'aek ie yo?	*What is the book he is reading?*
Kŭ saram i ponŭn ch'aek ŭl na to pwasse yo.	*I too have read the book he is reading.*

For some verbs *does* is a better translation than *is doing*:

Sat'ang ŭl choha hanŭn saekssi	*A girl who likes candy.*
Chip e tora kako sip'ŏ hanŭn ai	*The child who wants to go home.*

Notice that the -**nŭn** modifier form is not used with DESCRIPTION verbs (*is something*)—these have only the -**ŭn** form. This is why the -**ŭn** modifier comes out with two different translations : ' *which* HAS DONE ' for process verbs, ' *which* IS ' for description verbs. You will sometimes be in doubt whether a particular verb is a process or a description ; but the English translation usually tells you.

Isse yo and **ŏpse yo** are a bit strange ; they sometimes behave like description verbs, sometimes like process verbs. The forms **issŭn** and **ŏpsŭn** are rare, however : one usually hears only **innŭn** ...... *that exists, that someone has* and **ŏmnŭn** ...... *that is non-existent, that someone doesn't have*.

Here is a list of some typical verb bases with their modifier forms :

MEANING	BASE	-ŭn	-nŭn
I. CONSONANT BASES			
catches	chab-	chabŭn	chamnŭn
is high	nop'-	nop'ŭn	—
is nonexistent	ŏps-	(ŏpsŭn)	ŏmnŭn
closes	tad-	tadŭn	tannŭn
is like	kat'-	kat'ŭn	—
laughs	us-	usŭn	unnŭn
exists	iss-	(issŭn)	innŭn
finds	ch'aj-	ch'ajŭn	channŭn
washes	ssich'-	ssich'ŭn	ssinnŭn
reads	ilg-	ilgŭn	ingnŭn
loses	ilh-	ilhŭn	illŭn
licks	halt'-	halt'ŭn	hallŭn
steps on	palb-	palbŭn	pamnŭn
chants	ŭlp'-	ŭlp'ŭn	ŭmnŭn
puts	noh-	nohŭn	nonnŭn
eats	mŏg-	mŏgŭn	mŏngnŭn
cuts	kkakk-	kkakkŭn	kkangnŭn
shampoos	kam-	kamŭn	kamnŭn
is young	chŏlm-	chŏlmŭn	—
wears on feet	sin-	sinŭn	sinnŭn
sits	anj-	anjŭn	annŭn
breaks	kkŭnh-	kkŭnhŭn	kkŭnnŭn
II. VOWEL BASES			
is, equals	(i)-	(i)-n	—
honorific	-(ŭ)si-	-(ŭ)sin	-(ŭ)sinŭn
rests	swi-	swin	swinŭn
becomes	toe-	toen	toenŭn
pays	nae-	naen	naenŭn
writes	ssŭ-	ssŭn	ssŭnŭn
goes	ka-	kan	kanŭn
gives	chu-	chun	chunŭn
sees, reads	po-	pon	ponŭn
does	ha-	han	hanŭn
calls	purŭ-	purŭn	purŭnŭn

(98)

III. -w BASES

helps	**tow-**	**toun**	**tomnŭn**
lies	**nuw-**	**nuun**	**numnŭn**
is near	**kakkaw**	**kakkaun**	—
is pretty	**kow-**	**koun**	—

IV. -r BASES

walks	**kŏr-**	**kŏrŭn**	**kŏnnŭn**
listens	**tŭr-**	**tŭrŭn**	**tŭnnŭn**

V. l-EXTENDING VOWEL BASES

hangs	**kŏ-l-**	**kŏn**	**kŏnŭn**
enters	**tŭ-l-**	**tŭn**	**tŭnŭn**

Lesson 37

EXPERIENCES: " EVER ", " NEVER ", AND " SOMETIMES "

The modifier forms are used in a number of handy
expressions best learned as units:

-ŭn il i isse yo	*has done, (once) did, has done indeed*
-ŭn il i issŏsse yo	*had ever, once had done*
-ŭn il i ŏpse yo	*has never, never did*
-ŭn il i ŏpsŏsse yo	*had never, never had done*

The noun **il** means *work, job* but it also means *act,
experience*—so the literal meaning of the above expressions is something like *the act or experience of
having done something exists (or doesn't exist)*. Here
are some examples:

Han-guk ŭmsik ŭl mŏ-gŏ pon il i isse yo?	*Have you ever tried eating Korean food?*
Isse yo.	*Yes, I have.*
Han-guk ŭmsikchŏm e ka sŏ mŏgŭn il i isse yo.	*Yes, I have. I've been to a Korean restaurant to eat.*
Kŭ kongwŏn e sŏ san-ppo han il i isse yo?	*Have you ever taken a walk in that park?*
Ŏje kkaji nŭn kŏgi sŏ sanppo han il i ŏp-sŏtchi man, ŏje ppam e kŏgi ka sŏ sanppo haesse yo.	*Up to yesterday I hadn't ever taken a walk in that park, but yesterday I went there and took a walk.*
Kŭ chŏn e, Han-guk ai hago kach'i non il i ŏpsŏsse yo. Ch'ŏŭm iŏsse yo.	*Before that I had never played with a Korean child. It was (for) the first time.*
Han-guk yŏja rŭl man-nan il i ŏpsŏ sŏ, han saram mannago sip'ŏ yo.	*I've never met a Korean wo-man, so I'd like to meet one.*
Miguk yŏnghwa rŭl pon il i ŏpse yo?	*Haven't you ever seen an American movie?*
Wae uri rŭl ch'ajŭsin il i ŏpse yo?	*Why haven't you ever looked us up?*
Kŭrŏk'e koun ŭmak ŭl tŭrŭn il i ŏpse yo.	*I've never heard such pretty music.*

Now learn the following expressions:

-nŭn il i isse yo	*sometimes does, does indeed (on occasion)*
-nŭn il i issŏsse yo	*sometimes did, would indeed do*
-nŭn il i ŏpse yo	*never does, doesn't ever do*
-nŭn il i ŏpsŏsse yo	*never would do, never used to do*

These expressions mean literally *the act or experience of doing exists (or does not exist)*. Here are some examples:

Kŭ ttal i pyŏngjŏng hago yaegi rŭl hanŭn il i isse yo.	*His daughter sometimes talks with soldiers.*
Yaegi rŭl hanŭn il i itchi man, pyŏngjŏng hago sanppo hanŭn il i ŏpse yo.	*She sometimes talks, but she doesn't ever take walks with soldiers.*
Tambae rŭl p'inŭn il i itchi man, sul ul masinŭn il i ŏpse yo.	*She sometimes smokes, but she never drinks.*
Nae ga mannan yŏja nŭn tambae rŭl p'inŭn il i ŏpsŏtchi man, sul ŭl masinŭn il i issŏsse yo.	*The girl I met never smoked, but she sometimes drank.*
Sul ŭl nŏmu mŏgŏ sŏ, cha ppŏrinŭn il i issŏsse yŏ.	*She sometimes drank so much she'd fall asleep.*
Nae ga sul ŭl masinŭn il i itchi man, nŏmu mas(y)ŏ sŏ cha ppŏrin il i ŏpse yo.	*sometimes drink, but I've never drunk so much I've fallen asleep.*

Lesson 38

"BEFORE" AND "AFTER"
AND "WHILE"

To say *before something happens* or *before something happened* you use the **-ki** form followed by chŏn *prior, earlier, before, ago* usually followed by the particle **e**:

Hakkyo e ogi chŏn e kongbu rŭl hae nohasse yo.	*I studied the lesson before I came to school.*
Pi ga ogi chŏn e chip e tora ka ya hae yo.	*I've got to get home before it rains.*
Yaegi rŭl sijak hagi chŏn e, mul ŭl masŏsse yo.	*Before beginning my speech I took a drink of water.*
Taek e sŏ na kasigi chŏn e, na hant'e chŏnhwa rŭl hae chusipsio.	*Please phone me before you leave (go out of) your house.*

To say *after something happens* or *after something happened* you use the ordinary modifier form **-ŭn + hu** *afterward* which may be followed by the particle **e**:

Chip e tora on hu (e), kongbu rŭl haesse yo.	*I studied after I came home.*

Uri ga ŭmak ŭl tŭrŭn hu e, tapang e ka sŏ hongch'a rŭl han chan masŏsse yo.	*After we had heard the music, we went to a teashop and drank a cup of (black) tea.*
Uri kae ga chugŭ ppŭrin hu e, ai tŭl i orae ttongan urŏsse yo.	*After our dog died, the children cried for a long time.*
(Orae *long time.*	Tongan *interval*.)
Yŏngwa rŭl pon hu e, ŏsŏ chip e tora osipsio.	*Come right back home after you see the movie.*
Sŏnsaeng i chasin hu e tojŏk i tŭrŏ wasse yo, chasigi chŏn e tŭrŏ wasse yo ?	*Did the thief come in after you had gone to bed, (or) before you went to bed?*

To say *while something is happening* you use the processive modifier -nŭn followed by **chung** *midst of*, **tongan** *interval*, or **sai** (sae) *interval*. The particle **e** may follow :

Chanŭn chung iŏsse yo.	*It was while we were sleeping.*
Sŏnsaeng i yaegi rŭl hanŭn tongan (e), nae ga chal tŭtko issŏsse yo.	*While you were talking I was listening closely (well).*
Na nŭn chigŭm kongbu hanŭn chung iji man, kongbu han hu e uri ga sanppo hae to choha yo.	*I am now in the midst of studying, but after I've studied we can take a walk.*
Sŏnsaeng i sanppo hanŭn sai e, son nim i chip e osŏsse yo.	*While you were walking a guest came to the house.*
Sowi ga chanŭn sai, ttal i set'ak ŭl hae tŭryŏsse yo.	*While you (Lieutenant) were asleep, my daughter did your laundry for you.*

Lesson 39

FUTURE

The ordinary present form of verbs often has a
future meaning:

Nae ga hakkyo e ka yo.	*I'm going to school.*
Onŭl ppam kŭ il ŭl hae yo.	*I'll do that job tonight.*

But if you want to make the future specific, or if
you want to refer to a probable present (especially
with adjectives), you can use the **-kesse yo** form.

This **-kesse yo** (or **-gesse yo**) is added to the verb
base in the same way **-ko** and **-ki** are added:

Pi ga ogi chŏn e usan ŭl sa (noha) ya hagesse yo.	*I'll have to buy an umbrella before it rains.*
Miguk kyŏngch'i nŭn chok'esse yo.	*The scenery must be (is probably) nice in America.*
Muŏs ŭl mŏkkesse yo?	*What will we eat?*
Miguk e tora kasin hu e, muŏs ŭl hasigesse yo.	*What will you do when you get back to America?*
Ŏdi sasigesse yo?	*Where will you live?*
Ŏnje Han-guk e tora ogesse yo?	*When will you return to Korea?*

Notice the difference between **Chikkong i chigŭm**

(104)

il ŭl hago itkesse yo *The factory-hand must be working now* and **Chikkong i chigŭm il ŭl hae ya hae yo** *The factory-hand must work now.* Sometimes *must* means *likely, probably*; sometimes it means *has to*.

There is also a FUTURE MODIFIER form meaning ...... *that will do* or ...... *that someone will do* or ...... *that is to be done*:

Ssŭl p'yŏnji ga isse yo.	*I have letters to write.*
I il ŭl hal (s)saram i isse yo?	*Is there someone (a person) to do this job?*
Nae ga anhae hal (s)saram ŭl ch'atko isse yo.	*I'm looking for someone to show me around (guide me).*
Posil (k)kŏs i muŏs ie yo?	*What are you (going) to see?*
Mannasil (p)pyŏngjŏng i Miguk (s)saram ie yo?	*Is the soldier you are going to see an American?*
Kŭ pyŏngjŏng hago yaegi hal (k)kŏs i kyŏlhon ie yo?	*Is marriage what you're going to talk about with the soldier?*
Mŏgŭl (k)kŏs i isse yo?	*Is there anything to eat?*
Nae ga mŏgŭl (k)kŏs i itkesse yo?	*Would there (likely) be anything for me to eat?*
Sŏnsaeng i chapsusil (k)kŏs i issŭse yo?	*Do you have anything (for you) to eat, sir?*
Hasa ga set'ak hal (k)kŏs i itkesse yo?	*Do (would) you have any laundry to be done, corporal?*
Set'ak hal (s)saram i isse yo?	*Do you have someone to do the laundry?*
Set'ak hal (k)kŏs i isse yo?	*Do you (they) have a place to do the laundry?*

The ending of the future modifier form is **-ŭl** after

a consonant base, **-l** after a vowel base. Here are some typical verb types, with future and future modifier forms:

MEANING	BASE	-kesse yo	-ŭl / -l
I. CONSONANT BASES			
catches	chab-	chapkesse yo	chabŭl
is high	nop'-	nopkesse yo	nop'ŭl
is nonexistent	ŏps-	ŏpkesse yo	ŏpsŭl
closes	tad-	tatkesse yo	tadŭl
is like	kat'-	katkesse yo	kat'ŭl
laughs	us-	utkesse yo	usŭl
exist	iss-	itkesse yo	issŭl
finds	ch'aj-	chatkesse yo	ch'ajŭl
washes	ssich'-	ssitkesse yo	ssich'ŭl
reads	ilg-	ilkkesse yo / ikkesse yo	ilgŭl
loses	ilh-	ilk'esse yo	ilhŭl
licks	halt'-	halkkesse	halt'ŭl
steps on	palb-	palkkesse yo	palbŭl
chants	ŭlp'-	ŭpkesse yo	ŭlp'ŭl
puts	noh-	nok'esse yo	nohŭl
eats	mŏg-	mŏkkesse yo	mŏgŭl
cuts	kkakk-	kkakkesse yo	kkakkŭl
shampoos	kam-	kamkkesse yo	kamŭl
is young	chŏlm-	chŏmkkesse yo	chŏlmŭl
wears on feet	sin-	sinkkesse yo	sinŭl
sits	anj-	ankkesse yo	anjŭl
breaks	kkŭnh-	kkŭnk'esse yo	kkŭnhŭl
II. VOWEL BASES			
is, equals	(i)-	(i)-kesse yo	(i)-l
honorific	-(ŭ)si-	-(ŭ)sigesse yo	-(ŭ)sil
rests	swi-	swigesse yo	swil
becomes	toe-	toegesse yo	toel
pays	nae-	naegesse yo	nael
writes	ssŭ-	ssŭgesse yo	ssŭl

goes	ka-	kagesse yo	kal
gives	chu-	chugesse yo	chul
sees	po-	pogesse yo	pol
does	ha-	hagesse yo	hal
calls	purŭ-	purŭgesse yo	purŭl

III. -w BASES

helps	tow-	topkesse yo	toul
lies down	nuw-	nupkesse yo	nuul
is near	kakkaw-	kakkapkesse yo	kakkaul
is pretty	kow-	kopkesse yo	koul

IV. -r BASES

walks	kŏr-	kŏtkesse yo	kŏrŭl
listens	tŭr-	tŭtkesse yo	tŭrŭl

V. l-EXTENDING VOWEL BASES

hangs	kŏ-l-	kŏlgesse yo	kŏl
enters	tŭ-l-	tŭlgesse	tŭl

Lesson 40

" KNOWS " AND " CAN "

To say someone *knows* something or someone, you
use the verb **arŏ yo** (a-l-) ; the negative of this is a
special verb, **molla yo** (morŭ-) *does not know.* These
verbs are often used with the FUTURE **-kesse yo**, even
though the English translation uses the present :

Sŏnsaeng i asigesse yo ? *Do you know?*
Na nŭn kŭ saram ŭl *I don't know him but I know*
morŭgetchi man, kŭ *his father.*
saram abŏji rŭl alges-
se yo.

You will recall that the future sometimes means just a PROBABLE PRESENT. Notice the deferential way in English we say:

Kich'a ga ttŏnal ssikan ŭl asikesse yo?	*Would you know what time the train leaves?*
Sŏul e tahŭl ssikan ŭl mo-rŭgesse yo.	*I wouldn't know what time it gets to Seoul.*

(Ttŏna- *leave*, tah- *arrive*.)

To say someone *knows* THAT something happened, you say someone *knows the* FACT (kŏt) that something happened:

Kich'a ga pŏlssŏ ttŏnan kŏs ŭl asigesse yo?	*Do you know (realize) that the train has already left?*
Kŭ saram i chŏnjaeng chŏn e yŏgi on kŏs ŭl morŭsigesse yo.	*You don't know that he came here before the war.*

The verb **arŏ yo** sometimes means *realizes, finds out*:

Nae ga kŭ p'yŏnji rŭl ssŭn kŏs ŭl nugu hant'e sŏ arŏsse yo.	*From whom did you find out I wrote that letter?*

To say someone *knows* HOW TO do something, you use the future modifier -ŭl followed by the word **tchul** and **arŏ yo**:

Yŏng-ŏ rŭl hal tchul ase yo?	*Do you know how to speak English? Can you speak English?*
Han-guk mal ŭl chal hal tchul molla yo.	*I don't know how to speak Korean very well.*

| Han-gŭl ŭl ssŭl tchul moŭji man, kongbu hago sip'ŏ sŏ, chom karŭch'ŏ chusipsio. | *I don't know how to write Korean script (Han-gŭl) but I want to study it, so please teach (karŭch'i-) me a little.* |
| Heŏm-ch'il tchul ase yo? | *Do you know how to swim?* |

(Heŏm-ch'i- *swim*, heŏm-ch'ŏ yo *swims*.)

You will notice that this expression -ŭl tchul arŏ yo (and its negative -ŭl tchul molla yo) is sometimes translated *knows how to* (*doesn't know how to*) and sometimes *can* (*can't*).

This is a special meaning of the English word *can*; the more general meaning *is able to, is in a position to* is expressed in Korean by the expression: -ŭl ssu isse yo. The literal meaning of this expression is something like *there exists the possibility to do*:

Onŭl ppam e uri chip e osil ssu isse yo?	*Can you come to our house this evening?*
Han-gŭl ŭl ssŭl tchul alji man, mannyŏnp'il ina pus i ŏpsŏ sŏ, chikkŭm ssŭl ssu ŏpse yo.	*I know how to write Korean letters but I haven't a pen or a writing-brush, so I can't write (them) right now.*
Sigan i ŏpsŏ sŏ, nŏng-nŏk kongbu hal ssu ŏpsŏsse yo.	*I didn't have any time, so I couldn't study enough.*
Sigan i itchi man, ton i ŏpsŏ sŏ, sŏnsaeng hago kach'i kŏri e kal ssu ŏpse yo.	*I've got the time, but I haven't any money, so I can't go to town with you.*

There is still a third meaning of *can*—the same as the word *may*:

Onŭl ppam nŭtke tora wa to kwaench'anhŏ yo.	*You can (may) come back late tonight (because you have my permission).*

Contrast this with:

Onŭl ppam nŭtke tora ol ssu isse yo.	*You can (are able to) come back late tonight (because the busses are running late).*

Here are some more examples of these expressions:

Onŭl ohu e nae ga sinae e ka ya hagetchi man, chadongch'a ro kal ssu itkesse yo?	*I have to go to the city this this afternoon, but will I be able to go by car?*
Chadongch'a han tae itchi man, unjŏn hal ssu innŭn saram i in-nŭn kŏs ŭl molla yo.	*There's a (one) car available, but I don't know that there is anyone who can drive it.*
Chungwi ga unjŏn hasil tchul ase yo?	*Do you know how to drive, Lieutenant?*
Molla yo. Chadongch'a rŭl unjŏn han il i ŏpsŏ sŏ, unjŏn hal tchul molla yo.	*No I don't. I've never driven a car, so I don't know how.*
Kŭrŏch'i man, kŭ pyŏngjŏng i unjŏn hal tchul algesse yo.	*But that soldier probably knowns how to drive.*
Chŏnjaeng chŏn e t'ŭrŏk unjŏnsu ga ani -yŏsse yo?	*Wasn't he a truck driver be- fore the war?*

Lesson 41

PROBABLE FUTURE

The ordinary future -kesse yo means either DEFINITE
FUTURE or PROBABLE PRESENT. For a probable future
(*something probably will happen*) you use the expression -ŭl kkŏs ie yo which has a literal meaning somewhat like *it is the likely fact for something to happen*.
The word kŏt which has so many meanings — *thing,
fact, likely fact, that*—is often shortened to kŏ, and
the shortened expression -ŭl kkŏ -e yo is usually run
together to sound like -ŭl kke yo. Here are some
examples of both the full form and the abbreviated
form:

will probably catch	chabŭl kkŏs ie yo	chabŭl kke yo
will probably eat	mogŭl kkŏs ie yo	mogŭl kke yo
will probably read	ilgŭl kkŏs ie yo	ilgŭl kke yo
will probably come	ol kkŏs ie yo	ol kke yo
someone honored will probably do	hasil kkŏs ie yo	hasil kke yo
will probably live	sal kkŏs ie yo	sal kke yo

This probable future is seldom used of one's own
actions:

Chŏnjaeng hu e Kim sŏnsaeng i Wŏnsan e sal kke yo. Na nŭn Sŏul e salgesse yo.	*After the war Mr. Kim will probably live in Wonsan. I'll live in Seoul.*
Naeil nun i ol kke yo.	*Tomorrow it will probably snow (snow will probably come).*

(111)

Lesson 42

"WHEN" AND "IF"

There are a number of ways to translate the English word *when*. The most general is perhaps -ŭl ttae *(at) the time when*. The verb in front of ttae *time* is always in the future modifier form regardless of the tense of the English verb:

Chŏnjaeng i irŏnal ttae, nae ga Ilbon e salgo issŏsse yo.	*At the time the war broke out I was living in Japan.*
Kŭ ttae sŏnsaeng i ŏdi kesŏsse yo.	*Where were you then (at that time)?*
Pi ga ol ttae usan i issŏ ya hae yo.	*When it rains you have to have an umbrella.*
Kim sŏnsaeng ŭi chip e kal ttae, Han-guk mal man hasipsio.	*When we go to Mr. Kim's house, please talk only Korean.*

To say *if* you use a special verb form which has the shape -myŏn after a consonant base, -ŭmyŏn after a vowel base. This is also used to mean *whenever*:

Pi ga omyŏn, nae ga chip e itkesse yo.	*If it rains, I'll stay home.*

Pi ga omyŏn, nae ga chip e isse yo.	*Whenever it rains, I stay home.*
Abŏji ga chŏnyŏk e chip e tora omyŏn, ai tŭl i choha hae yo.	*The children are glad when their father comes home in the evening.*

There's a special way to say *when one thing happens then something else interrupts it*—sentences like *when I was listening to the radio, I heard a noise upstairs* or *while we were out walking it rained*.

You use a form which ends in **-ta** (or **-da**) and is usually followed by the particle **ga**. This shows the single interruption of an action—which may or may not be resumed. **Nae ga radio rŭl tŭtta ga, u ch'ŭng e sori rŭl tŭrŏsse yo. Uri ga sanppo hada ga, pi ga wasse yo.**

There is a past form of this **-ta** which has the ending **-ŏtta** (or **-atta** with a number of irregularities, like all infinitives and past forms). The meaning of the past **-ŏtta** form is *when one thing has happened, then something else contradictory or unanticipated happens right after*—without INTERRUPTING the action so much as CHANGING it. For example:

Sangjŏm e katta wasse yo.	*I went to the store and then (turned around and) came right back.*
Kim sŏnsaeng i up'yŏn-guk e watta kasse yo.	*Mr Kim came to the post office and left again.*

Two contradictory actions can be shown as going on in ALTERNATION by using two of these **-ŏtta** forms followed by **hae yo**:

Saram i katta watta   *People keep coming and going.*
hae yo.

To talk about two actions which are not in alternation, but are going on at the same time, you use the
-ŭmyŏn form followed by the particle sŏ :

Radio rŭl tŭrŭmyŏn sŏ   *I study while listening to the*
kongbu hae yo.   *radio.*
Ch'aek ŭl pomyŏn sŏ   *I read (books) while baby-*
aegi rŭl pwa yo.   *sitting.*

Sometimes the -ŭmyŏn sŏ form means *even though*
(the same as -ŏ to) just as the English *while* can have
that meaning :

Han-guk mal ŭl kongbu   *While (though) I am studying*
hamyŏn sŏ, chal hal   *Korean, I can't speak it*
tchul molla yo.   *very well.*

You may find this a handy tag translation for the
-ta (ga) forms : BUT *then (something else happens)*.

You will recall that -ŏ sŏ means *does and then* or
does and so, and -ko means *does and then* or *does
and also*.

The important thing about the -ta (ga) forms is
that they always show a TRANSFER of action. The
gerund -ko simply links two verb expressions ; -ta
(ga) links two verb expressions stressing the CONTRA-
DICTORY nature of the two ; -ŏ sŏ stressed the close
CONSEQUENCE of the second verb.

Here are the -ŭmyŏn and -ta (ga) forms for some
typical verbs :

MEANING	BASE	-ŭmyŏn -myŏn	-ta (ga)	-ŏtta (ga)
I. CONSONANT BASES				
catches	chab-	chabŭmyŏn	chapta (ga)	chabŏtta (ga)
closes	tad-	tadŭmyŏn	tatta (ga)	tadŏtta (ga)
exists	iss-	issŭmyŏn	itta (ga)	issŏtta (ga)
is non-existent	ŏps-	ŏpsŭmyŏn	ŏpta (ga)	ŏpsŏtta (ga)
laughs	us-	usŭmyŏn	utta (ga)	usŏtta(ga)
finds	ch'aj-	ch'aj-ŭmyŏn	ch'atta (ga)	ch'ajŏtta (ga)
reads	ilg-	ilgŭmyŏn	ikta (ga)	ilgŏtta (ga)
puts	noh-	nohŭmyŏn	not'a (ga)	nohatta (ga)
eats	mŏg-	mŏgŭmyŏn	mŏkta (ga)	mŏgŏtta (ga)
wears on feet	sin-	sinŭmyŏn	sintta (ga)	sinŏtta (ga)
sits	anj-	anjŭmyŏn	antta (ga)	anjŏtta (ga)
breaks	kkŭnh-	kkŭnh-ŭmyŏn	kkŭnt'a (ga)	kkŭnhŏt-ta (ga)
II. VOWEL BASES				
rests	swi-	swimyŏn	swida (ga)	swiŏtta (ga)
pays	nae-	naemyŏn	naeda (ga)	naetta(ga)
writes	ssŭ-	ssŭmyŏn	ssŭda (ga)	ssŏtta (ga)
goes	ka-	kamyŏn	kada (ga)	katta (ga)
does	ha-	hamyŏn	hada (ga)	haetta(ga)
calls	purŭ-	purŭmyŏn	purŭda (ga)	pullŏtta (ga)
III. -w BASES				
helps	tow-	toumyŏn	topta (ga)	towatta (ga)

(115)

lies down	nuw-	nuumyŏn	nupta (ga)	nuwŏtta (ga)
is near	kakkaw-	kakkau-myŏn	kakkapta (ga)	kakka-wŏtta (ga)

IV. -r BASES

walks	kŏr-	kŏrŭmyŏn	kŏtta (ga)	kŏrŏtta (ga)
listens	tŭr-	tŭrŭmyŏn	tŭtta (ga)	tŭrŏtta (ga)

V. l- EXTENDING VOWEL BASES

hangs	kŏ-l-	kŏlmyon	kŏlda (ga)	kŏrŏtta (ga)
enters	tŭ-l-	tŭlmyŏn	tŭlda (ga)	tŭrŏtta (ga)

Lesson 43

HOPING AND WISHING

To say *I hope something will happen* or *I wish something would happen* you use an expression which means literally *if something happens it will be nice*: -ŭmyon chok'esse yo.

Nun i omyŏn chok'esse yo.	*I hope it snows.*
Abŏji ga chip e tora omyŏn chok'esse yo.	*I wish Father would come home.*
Ttal ŭl manna to cho-hŭmyon chok'esse yo.	*I hope I may meet your daughter.*
Ilbon e to ka pol ssu issŭmyon chok'esse yo.	*I hope I'll be able to go see Japan, too.*

Han-guk mal ŭl Han-guk (s)saram kach'i chal hamyŏn chok'esse yo.	*I wish I could talk Korean well like the Koreans.*
Pi ga an omyŏn chok'esse yo.	*I hope it doesn't rain.*
Uri chip e osil ssu issŭmyon chok'esse yo.	*It'll be nice if you can come to our house.*
Naeil kkaji yŏgi issŭmyon chok'esse yo. Nae ga issŏ to choha yo?	*I hope I can stay here till tomorrow. May I stay?*

To say *I would like to do* you use -ko sip'ŏ yo:

Kŏri e kago sip'ŏ yo.	*I'd like to go to town.*

But to say *I would like* YOU *to do something* you say something like *I would be grateful if you would*:

I os ŭl ppalmyŏn komapkesse yo.	*I would like you to wash these clothes.*

To say *someone would like to do something* you say -ko sip'ŏ hae yo:

Ŏmŏni ga swigo sip'ŏ hae yo.	*Mother would like to rest.*

But to say *someone would like* SOMEONE ELSE *to do something* you say -ŭmyŏn komawŏ hagesse yo:

Ttal i kŭrŭs ŭl ssich'ŭmyŏn ŏmŏni ga komawŏ hagesse yo.	*Mother would like daughter to wash the dishes.*
Sŏnsaeng i yŏgi kesimyŏn abŏji ga komawŏ hagesse yo.	*Father would like you to stay here.*

(117)

To GIVE permission you say **-ǒ to choha yo** (or **-ǒ to kwaench'anhǒ yo**) *it is OK to, it is all right even if (you do)*.

To DENY permission, you use the expression **-ǔmyǒn an toe yo** *it won't do to, one mustn't, oughtn't, shouldn't*. For the special meaning *won't do* you can use **mot ssǒ yo** *can't be used* instead of **an toe yo** *does not become*:

Nǔtke tora omyǒn an toe yo.	*You mustn't come back late.*
Ai tǔl i tambae rǔl p'imyǒn mot ssǒ yo.	*Children shouldn't smoke cigarettes.*
Hwanja hago orae ttong-an yaegi rǔl hasi-myǒn mot ssǒ yo.	*You mustn't talk with the patient long.*
Sǒnsaeng i kǔrǒk'e sul ǔl masimyon mot ssǒ yo.	*You shouldn't drink so (much).*
Pi ga omyǒn mot ssǒ yo.	*It's no good if it rains.*

To say *has to, must* you use the expression **-ǒ ya hae yo**.

Iltchigi tora osǒ ya hae yo.	*You have to come back early.*

But a milder way to expressing obligation is *ought* or *should* which the Koreans say with **-chi anhǔmyon an toe yo** *if you don't, it's no good*:

Iltchigi tora osiji an-hǔmyon an toe yo.	*You should come back early.*

Kim sŏnsaeng chip e kagi chŏn e pap ŭl mŏkchi anhŭmyon mot ssŏ yo.	We ought to eat before we go to Mr. Kim's house.
Kich'a ga ttŏnagi chŏn e ŭmsing-mul chom sa noch'i anhŭmyon an toe yo.	We ought to buy some food (stuffs) before the train leaves.
Pyŏnso e an kamyŏn an toe yo.	I ought to go to the bathroom.

Lesson 44

WHAT THE WEATHER LOOKS LIKE

To say something *looks like* or *seems like* something you can use several expressions. One consists of any modifier form followed by **moyang ie yo** *it's the appearance of.* Another consists of any modifier form followed by **kŏt kat'e yo** *it's like the fact of.* The former expression stresses the appearance; the latter stresses the similarity:

| Kisaeng in moyang ie yo. | She looks like a geisha. |
| Kisaeng in kŏt kat'e yo. | She seems to be a geisha. |

Here are some examples of these expressions:

| Pi ga ol moyang ie yo. | It looks as if it would rain. |
| Ŏje ppam nun i on moyang ie yo. | It looks as though it had snowed last night. |

Nal i chohǔn kǒt kat'e yo.	The weather seems to be nice.
Nal i nappǔn kǒt kat'e yo.	The weather seems to be bad (nasty).
Hanǔl e kurǔm i issǒ sǒ, ǒduwǒ yo.	There are clouds in the sky, so it's dark.
Hanǔl e kurǔm i issǒ sǒ ǒdupchi man, hae ga na onǔn moyang ie yo.	There are clouds in the sky, so it's dark, but it looks like the sun is coming out.
Hae ga na wa sǒ, palgǒ yo.	The sun is out, so it's light.
Onǔl ach'im param i punǔn moyang ie yo? Param i nǒmu pulmyǒn, os i ttǒrǒjil kke yo.	Does there seem to be a wind blowing this morning? If it blows too much (hard), the clothes will (likely) fall down.
Aegi ga yuri-(t)chan ǔl ttǒrǒt'ǔrin kǒt kat'e yo.	The baby seems to have dropped the glass.

To say that something *gets to be*, *turns into* a certain condition, you use the infinitive of an adjective followed by the auxiliary verb chǒ yo (base chi-). This auxiliary verb is usually linked directly to the infinitive so it sounds like jǒ yo (ji-):

Ttǔgǒwǒ chǒsse yo.	It's gotten hot.
Ttǔgǒwǒ yo.	It is hot.
Sǒnǔl hae chimyǒn, nae ga tora ka yo.	I'll go back when it gets cool.
Sǒnǔl han kos ǔl ch'atko isse yo.	I'm looking for a cool spot.
Hae ga na omyǒn, ttattǔt hae chǒ yo.	When the sun comes out it gets warm.

Yŏgi ga ttattŭt hago choha yo.	*This place is nice and warm.*
Os i tŏrŏwŏ chŏtchi man, nae ga os ŭl pparŏ sŏ, chigŭm kkaekkŭt hae yo.	*The clothes got dirty, but I washed them, so now they are clean.*

Lesson 45

"BECAUSE"

You have learned that **-ŏ sŏ** links two verbal expressions stressing that the second is the consequence of the first: *and so.* This is a very weak way of saying the second expression *is so* BECAUSE of the first. There are a number of ways in which this BECAUSE can be made a bit stronger.

The most common is to use the **-ki** form followed by **ttaemun (e)**:

Pi ga ogi ttaemun e, na nŭn kago sipchi anhŏ yo.	*I don't want to go because it's raining.*
Ton i ŏpki ttaemun e, Kim sŏnsaeng ŭn kago sip'ŏ haji anhŏ yo.	*Mr. Kim doesn't want to go because he hasn't any money.*

For the past and future there are special forms which consist of inserting the past marker (**-ŏss-** in its basic form) or the future marker (**-kess-** in its basic form) between the base and **-ki**: **-ŏtki** (**-atki**, etc.) and **-ketki** (**-getki** etc.) :

Nae ga pŏlssŏ pap ŭl mŏgŏtki ttaemun e, pae ga kop'ŭji anhŏ yo.	*I'm not hungry because I've already eaten.*
Nae ga naeil Kim sŏnsaeng ŭl mannagetki ttaemun e, kŭ i hant'e nae ga kŭ yaegi rŭl hagesse yo.	*I'll tell Mr Kim about that, because I'll see him tomorrow.*
Wae kŭrŏk'e nŭtke tora ose yo?	*Why do you come home so late?*
Kongjang e sŏ il ŭl manhi hae ya haetki ttaemun ie yo.	*It's because we had a lot of work to do at the factory.*

Another way to say *because* is to use a modifier form followed by **kkadalk** *reason*. This may be followed by **e** or **ŭro** with about the same meaning *for the reason that* or by **ie yo** with the meaning *it is for the reason that*, *it is because* :

Nun i nŏmu manhi onŭn kkadalk e, chadongch'a rŭl unjŏn hal ssu ŏpse yo.	*We can't drive the car because it is snowing so hard.*
Kŏrŏ ka ya hal kkadalk e, nŭtke tak'esse yo.	*We'll arrive late because we'll have to walk.*
Il ŭl manhi han kkadalk ŭro, p'igon hae yo.	*I'm tired because I had to work a lot.*
Wae kŭ yŏja rŭl choha hase yo? Ŏlgul i koun kkadalk ie yo?	*Why do you like that girl? Is it because she has a pretty face (...... her face is pretty)?*

Lesson 46

CASUAL REMARKS: -chi yo

You have learned that the **-chi** form appears in negative sentences (**-chi anhŏ yo** *does not, is not*) and at the end of clauses with the particle **man** (**-chi man** *does but, is but*).

This form also appears at the end of a sentence before the polite particle **yo**. The meaning of a sentence ending in **-chi yo** (or **-ji yo**) is about the same as one ending in **-ŏ yo**—this is just a more CASUAL way of putting the sentence.

These casual sentences are frequently mixed with ordinary sentences and sometimes the casual flavor gives them rather special meanings. For one thing, these are about the only sentences that occur with that peculiar dipping intonation you may have noticed with the expression **Ani yo** *No.*

The meaning of this dipping intonation is to LIVEN UP the sentence or to INSIST on it ; often the sentence is a sort of question, and the meaning is ...... *it is, isn't it?* or *does, doesn't it?* :

Kim sŏnsaeng isiji yo?	*You are Mr Kim, aren't you?*
Yŏgi chom swiŏ to cho-ch'i yo?	*It'll be all right to rest here a bit won't it?*

Often the -chi yo form is a COMMAND or PROPOSITION, offered somewhat casually. This is especially frequent when the verb is honorific:

Ch'a han chan masiji yo?	*Shall we have a cup of tea? Let's have a cup of tea.*
Iri osiji yo.	*Come this way.*
Yŏgi anjŭsiji yo.	*Sit here.*
Chom kidarisiji yo!	*Wait just a moment.*
Yŏnghwa rŭl posiji yo?	*Shall we go to a movie? Let's see a movie.*

Sometimes the -chi yo form is a question, again rather casual:

Sŏnsaeng i kkoch' ŭl choha hasiji yo?	*Do you like flowers? I suppose you like flowers?*
Miguk e ŏnje tora ka-siji yo?	*When will you be going back to America?*

If the -chi form is a statement about someone else, the English translation can suggest the flavor of the casualness by adding a rather meaningless *you-know* or *don't-you-know* or *I-guess*.

Often this is a way of GIVING INFORMATION in Korean —the casualness has a polite tinge:

Miguk e to ch'uun nal i itchi yo.	*We have cold days (or weather) in America too, you know.*
Brown sowi ga Chicago sŏ salji yo.	*Lt. Brown lives in Chicago.*
Nae ga pyŏngjŏng i ani -ji yo. Kunsok iji yo.	*I'm not a soldier, you know. I'm a civilian (employee of the army—DAC), you see.*

| Chŏnjaeng chŏn e uri tongni ga chohatchi yo. | *Before the war, our village was rather nice.* |
| Kŭ pyŏngjŏng i Han-guk (s)saram iji yo? Mullon iji yo! | *Is that soldier a Korean? Of course!* |

You do not usually answer questions about yourself with the **-chi yo** form. Use the ordinary **-ŏ yo** form instead.

Lesson 47

SOME VARIANTS

The one thing which perhaps impresses you most is that no two Koreans seem to talk the same way. There are a great many local dialects in Korea, and these differ from each other much more than local dialects in America. In addition, the same person will often say the same word in three or four different ways, just as one and the same American may some-times say ICE*cream* and sometimes *ice*CREAM, sometimes *do not* and sometimes *don't*, sometimes *would you* and sometimes *wouldja*. You have already leaned a few of these variants. Here are some more.

In many parts of Korea, especially in the North, people differentiate certain words by vowel length. The word for *snow* (**nun**) is pronounced longer than

the word for *eye* (**nun**). There are really quite a few
minimal pairs in which this vowel length makes a
difference, yet it is ignored in the ordinary speech of
many South Koreans.

The sound we write **oe** is usually pronounced like
we (as in *wet*), but some people pronounce it **wae** (as
in *Wac*) and others give it a special little twist which
makes it resemble the German or French **oe**.

The vowel **ŭ** is often dropped after another vowel:
taŭm *next* frequently sounds like **tam**; **ch'ŏŭm** *for
the first time* like **ch'ŏm**. The vowel **i** is sometimes
reduced to **y**: **p'iŏ yo** *smokes* often sounds like **p'yŏ
yo**. The vowel **u** is sometimes reduced to **w**: **chapsuŏ yo** *someone honored eats* often sounds like **chaps-
wŏ yo**, **hae chuŏ yo** *does for someone* like **hae chwŏ
yo**.

In Seoul the vowel **u** is freely substituted for **o** after
a consonant: **tun** for **ton** *money*; **chungi** for **chongi**
paper; **hagu** for **hago** *and*; **ch'atku** for **ch'atko** *looking for*; **na tu** for **na to** *me too*. Some of these **u**
forms have become so widespread as to be considered
standard: **haru** *one day* (originally **haro**), **sigul** *country,
rural area* (originally **sigol**).

Throughout much of the southern part of Korea
the vowel **ae** is distinguished from **e** poorly if at all,
especially when the syllable is not preceded by a
pause. There are only a few common contrasts such
as **nae** *my* and **ne** *your* (speaking to a child), **kae** *dog*
and **ke** *crab*, **ŏpse yo** *there aren't any* and **ŏpsae yo**
eliminates. As a result, you won't always be sure

whether you are hearing **ae** or **e**, but then many Koreans aren't sure either.

The sequences **hy** and **hi** are often replaced by **s** and **si** in dialects: **sŏ** for **hyŏ** *tongue*, **sim** for **him** *strength*. The vowel **e** varies freely with **i** in certain words: **che-il** or **chi-il** *number 1, most*, **ŏdi** or **ŏde** *where*.

Lesson 48

SOME ABBREVIATIONS

Here are some common shortened forms. **Kŏt** is shortened to **kŏ**, **kŏs i** to **ke**, and **kŏs ie yo** to **ke yo**. **I ke nae ke yo**=**I kŏs i nae kŏs ie yo.** *This is mine.*

Muŏt is shortened to **mwŏ** or **mŏ**, **muŏs i** to **m(u)e** and **muŏs ie yo** to **m(u)e yo.** **M(u)e isse yo?**=**Muŏs i isse yo?** *What do you have?* **M(u)e yo?** = **Muŏs ie yo?** *What is it?*

The particle **nŭn** is abbreviated to **n** after a vowel: **na n**=**na nŭn** *as for me*, **i kŏ n**=**i kŏs ŭn** *this thing*. The particle **rŭl** is abbreviated to **l** after a vowel: **na l**=**na rŭl** *me* (as direct object), **i kŏ l**=**i kŏs ŭl** *this thing* (as direct object).

You have already learned that **nugu** becomes **nu** in front of the particle **ga**, and that **na** becomes **nae** in that position. And you have learned that **ani** is shortened to **an** in front of a verb. You may run into other abbreviations from time to time; try to find out what the full form of the abbreviation is. If you show you haven't understood, a Korean will repeat himself and often give you an expanded version of an abbreviated expression just as we often repeat *do not* for *don't* when we slow down.

Lesson 49

THE STRUCTURE OF VERB FORMS

A complete description of Korean verbs is too involved for a textbook of this size. However, a general notion of the structure of the forms may be of help to you. Look at the following table which shows, in a rough way, how the verb forms are put together.

1 BASE	2 HONORIFIC	3 PAST	4 PAST	5 FUTURE	6 MOOD	(7) (PARTICLE)
	-(ŭ)s(i)-	-ŏss- -ass- etc.	-ŏss-	-kess-	-ŏ, -a, -e	(yo)
					-ko -ki -chi -(ŭ)myon etc.	

Now look at the forms on the next page:

1	2	3	4	5	6	(7)
Tad-					-ŏ	(yo)
Tat-				-kess-	-e	(yo)
Tad-		-ŏss-			-e	(yo)
Tad-	-ŭs-				-e	(yo)
Tad-		-ŏss-	-ŏss-		-e	(yo)
Tad-		-ŏt-		-kess-	-e	(yo)
Tad-		-ŏss-	-ŏt-	-kess-	-e	(yo)
Tad-	-ŭsi-			-gess-	-e	(yo)
Tad-	-ŭs-	-ŏss-			-e	(yo)
Tad-	-ŭs-	-ŏss-	-ŏss-		-e	(yo)
Tad-	-ŭs-	-ŏt-		-kess-	-e	(yo)
Tad-	-ŭs-	-ŏss-	-ŏt-	-kess-	-e	(yo)

These forms have the following meanings:

Tadŏ yo.	*Closes.*
Tatkesse yo.	*Will close. Probably closes.*
Tadŏsse yo.	*Closed.*
Tadŭse yo.	*Someone honored closes.*
Tadŏssŏsse yo.	*Had closed. Closed.*
Tadŏtkesse yo.	*Will have closed. Probably closed.*
Tadŏssŏtkesse yo.	*Will have closed. Probably had closed.*
Tadŭsigesse yo.	*Someone honored will close. Someone honored probably closes.*
Tadŭsŏsse yo.	*Someone honored closed.*
Tadŭsŏssŏsse yo.	*Someone honored had closed.*
Tadŭsŏtkesse yo.	*Someone honored will have closed. Someone honored probably closed.*
Tadŭsŏssŏtkesse yo.	*Someone honored will have closed. Someone honored probably had closed.*

The past-past (*had done, did*) and the past-future (*will have done, probably did*) are not often used.

There are quite a lot of *moods* (the final suffix in the verb form) and you have only learned a few of the most useful ones in this textbook.

Lesson 50

SOME MILITARY WORDS

kundan	*corps*
sadan	*division*
yŏndae	*regiment*
taedae	*battalion*
chungdae	*company*
sodae	*platoon*
pundae	*detachment*
pudae	*outfit, unit*
saryŏngbu	*headquarters*
wihŏm	*danger*
chu(ŭ)i	*caution, care*
anjŏn	*safety*
ŭ(i)sa	*doctor*
pyŏngwŏn	*hospital*
kiji	*(military) base*
pyŏng-yŏng	*military camp*
min-gan, si-min	*civilians*
p'okt'an	*bomb*
p'okkyŏk hae yo	*bombs (something)*
p'okkyŏkki	*bomber (plane)*

t'anhwan	*ammunition, shell*
sŏryu	*document*
Yŏnhapkuk	*United Nations*
Yŏnhapkun	*UN Troops*
chŏk-kun	*enemy forces*
kun	*forces*
chiroe	*land mine*
suroe	*underwater mine*
ch'ong	*gun*
soch'ong	*rifle*
kwŏnch'ong	*pistol*
chadong soch'ong	*automatic carbine*
taep'o	*(big) gun, cannon*
kigwanch'ong	*machine gun*
suryut'an	*hand grenade*
hwayŏm pangsagi	*flame thrower*
chŏnch'a	*tank*
yugyŏktae	*guerilla forces*
chŏngbo	*(military) intelligence*
chŭngmyŏng	*identification*
chŏnsŏn	*front line*
hwasŏn	*firing line*
wich'i	*location*
chido	*map*
p'yosik	*mark*
susŏnggi	*supply plane, cargo*
yak	*medicine*
hŏnbyŏng	*MP*
pogŭp	*supply*
pogŭp-pu	*quartermaster*
pimil	*secret*
kang	*river*
ch'ŏnmak	*tent*
kunbok	*uniform*
ŭ(i)bok	*clothes* (=ot)

yangbok	*clothes, suit, dress (American style)*
ch'ŏltchomang	*barbed wire*
p'oro	*Prisoner of War*
sŏnjŏn	*propaganda*

ROMANIZATION TABLE

ROMANIZATION TABLE

The following Romanization table compares the transliteration of the USUAL or BASIC values of the Korean letters. There are five columns.

The first shows the letters of the Korean alphabet, **Han-gŭl**. These are arranged not according to any traditional order, but according to their phonetic characteristics.

The next column presents the McCune-Reischauer transcription used in this book.

The third column shows the Yale Romanization used by the author in other publications on the Korean language. This system avoids the use of unusual symbols or gadgets over ordinary letters by taking advantage of certain principles built into the structure of the language. But it takes a little while to get used to the values of some of the spellings.

The fourth column gives the Romanization used by Fred Lukoff in his textbook *Spoken Korean* (2 vols, Henry Holt and Company; there is also an Armed Forces edition). This book contains a lot of excellent conversation practice and you might want to continue your study of Korean with it.

The last column shows the symbols used by Elinor Clark Horne in her book *Introduction to Spoken Korean* (2 vols., Far Eastern Publication, Yale University). This book is no longer in print.

Learning the shapes of native Korean symbols is just part of the job in learning to read and write; you will also need to know something about Korean spelling rules and the ways the symbols are put together to make syllables and words. Koreans will be glad to help you with this once you have learned something of the spoken language.

Hangŭl	McCune-R.	Yale	Lukoff	Horne
ㅂ	p, b	p	p	p
ㅍ	p'	ph	ph	ph, pph
ㅃ	pp	pp	pp	pp
ㄷ	t, d	t	t	t
ㅌ	t'	th	th	th, tth
ㄸ	tt	tt	tt	tt
ㅅ	s	s	s	s
ㅆ	ss	ss	ss	ss
ㅈ	ch, j	c	j	c
ㅊ	ch'	ch	jh	ch, tch
ㅉ	tch	cc	jj	tc
ㄱ	k, g	k	k	k
ㅋ	k'	kh	kh	kh, kkh
ㄲ	kk	kk	kk	kk
ㅁ	m	m	m	m
ㄴ	n	n	n	n
ㅇ	ng	ng	ng	ŋ

Hangŭl	McCune-R.	Yale	Lukoff	Horne
ㄹ	r, l	l	l	l
ㅎ	h	h	h	h
ㅣ	i	i	i	i
ㅟ	wi	wi	wi	wi
ㅔ	e	ey	e	e
ㅖ	ye	yey	ye	ye
ㅞ	we	wey	we	we
ㅚ	oe	oy	ö	we
ㅐ	ae	ay	ä	ɛ
ㅒ	yae	yay	yä	yɛ
ㅙ	wae	way	wä	wɛ
ㅡ	ŭ	u	tt	ə
ㅓ	ŏ	e	φ	ɔ
ㅕ	yŏ	ye	yφ	yɔ
ㅝ	wŏ	we	wφ	wɔ
ㅏ	a	a	a	a
ㅑ	ya	ya	ya	ya
ㅘ	wa	wa	wa	wa
ㅜ	u	*wu	u	u
ㅠ	yu	yu	yu	yu
ㅗ	o	o	o	o
ㅛ	yo	yo	yo	yo
ㅢ	ŭi	uy	tt, i, tti	əi

* but u after p, ph, pp, m, y